FORCE FABRIC

The nude figure defines the best way to learn the fundamentals of drawing, yet the end goal of most art presents clothed figures, be it animation, video games, film, or fine art. This seventh book in the 'FORCE' series instructs artists on understanding fabric with FORCE, thus leading to improved drawings of clothed figures. Expertly organized and beautifully illustrated, the book instructs artists to see clothing in a new way, through FORCE. Michael's clear, concise, and informal writing coupled with Mritunjay and Michael's FORCE drawings of clothed models comprehensibly informs you, the curious artist, to identify and draw FORCE clothing.

Key Features:

- The unique, dynamic FORCE Drawing learning system that has helped thousands of artists enhance their figure drawing abilities now brings clothing to the figure!
- Easy to follow fundamentals on drawing clothed figures for games, animation, film, or fine art
- A clear, organized, and understandable, step-by-step approach to learn about the effects of FORCE on fabric and how that pertains to drawing clothes
- Learn to see clothes through tight, medium, and loose-fit and discover the common fold types per category, making it easier to identify and draw
- A 'sticker system' that presents the different types of folds found in different fit types of clothing
- Each chapter has exercises you can use to help learn the process of drawing clothes
- Find out how line can illustrate the texture of different fabrics in your clothing drawings
- A robust author website with further information, forums, and videos
- Color-coded page edges to quickly find the material you need
- Unlock your imagination; put the theory into practice with detailed exercises to sharpen your skills

FORCE FABRIC

How to Draw Clothes

Written and Illustrated by Michael Mattesi

Illustrated by Mritunjay Varun

Visit www.drawingforce.com

Sign up for Mentorship

View online tutorials

Enroll in Classes and join the FORCE Community!

CRC Press
Taylor & Francis Group
Boca Raton London New York

CRC Press is an imprint of the
Taylor & Francis Group, an **informa** business

Designed cover image: Michael Mattesi

First edition published 2024
by CRC Press
2385 Executive Center Drive, Suite 320, Boca Raton, FL 33431

and by CRC Press
4 Park Square, Milton Park, Abingdon, Oxon, OX14 4RN

CRC Press is an imprint of Taylor & Francis Group, LLC

© 2024 Michael Mattesi

ISBN: 978-1-138-48546-4 (hbk)
ISBN: 978-1-138-48541-9 (pbk)
ISBN: 978-1-351-04946-7 (ebk)

DOI: 10.1201/9781351049467

Typeset in Futura
by codeMantra

Michael's Dedications

For Opi, my Polish grandfather, an incredibly skilled tailor. Above are German books for tailoring clothes and a wooden triangle, my cherished remnants of him and his trade. His skills helped him navigate through World War II, discover and marry my grandmother, become a father to my mother, and migrate to the United States to establish himself in his career.

My Italian grandmother, Nonna, chased the American dream, working for pennies stitching high-end Italian ties. She worked diligently to buy a house in Brooklyn and support their family.

Mritunjay's Dedication

To my beloved mother Jyoti Varun and grandmother, Gayatri Devi Varun, who have always been my source of inspiration and strength. Your unwavering love and support have guided me through every challenge and celebrated every victory. This book is dedicated to you, with gratitude and love, for shaping me into the person I am today. Thank you for being my rock and my shining star. I love you always.

Contents

Foreword

As a costume designer, I visualize and design all the costumes for films and television shows. I am responsible for creating the characters through clothing for audiences to understand who these people are, what economic background they come from and what is their emotional journey. As you see an actor on the screen you can tell immediately, before they say their dialogue, who they are by what clothing they are wearing. Clothing informs our eyes and tells a story.

I was extremely excited to read Mike Mattesi's book. I designed many CGI characters for films. I got to work with the director Rob Minkoff on Stuart Little, who upon hiring me told me he wanted Stuart to look like a normal human teenager. It was a challenging task as Stuart is a mouse and his body does not resemble the human body due to his big tail and giant ears.

In Mike's book, you can learn how to approach functional design of CG clothes. It was very informative to read the explanation how to do it step by step. Stuart's CGI costumes were difficult to design and I wish I had Mike's FORCE Fabric book to help me understand how to approach scale and proportion of designing for his Stuart's odd shape. The Force book will teach you how to find the right fit, how the fabric needs to move and feel like the real thing. As costume designers/creators we have to think of fabric movement, volume and memory—and all of that is in this book. Reading about the small detail that Mike explains about folds, wraps, seams and zippers will add to better design of an overall costume.

For Enchanted, the film directed by Kevin Lima, I had to design costumes for 2D characters, which turned into live action characters played by actors. In the case of the evil Maleficent, she transformed into a CGI dragon. I was dealing with designing in three mediums and had to translate the costumes, shapes, proportions and textures from a flat drawing to real life and then CGI, all seamlessly and accurately. In each medium, they had to move and feel the same. I loved the challenge and how important each detail was to make sure the characters looked perfect for each incarnation.

When we design CGI characters, we have to go through each step and Mike teaches you how to do it from beginning to end. When I finished designing Stuart's looks and was happy with the fit costume, I still needed to add texture and aging. This is a crucial stage to make the clothing look like real fabric and this FORCE book helps you understand that. Stuart had scuffed knees, some dirt on his shirt, and he did end up looking like a real teenager!

The FORCE Fabric book will help you learn how to create digital costumes that will feel as real as possible to the human eye and delight audiences who watch the films.

Enjoy! Mona May @itsmonamay

Special Thanks

Michael

The person I don't know how to thank deeply enough is my wife Ellen. Twenty-five years of marriage and a library of FORCE books later, she has been my inspiration, my support, my personal editor, and so many other facets in my life. I want all of you to know that all of these FORCE books would not exist without her.

To my editor at CRC press, Sean Connolly, whose unwavering trust and support keeps me inspired to write new books!

To SM Amudhapriya and the team at Codemantra for guiding the book through production to its successful completion.

To Mritunjay, for his faith in the FORCE drawing approach and helping me show new artists how amazing their drawings could be utilizing FORCE!

Mritunjay

To Mr. Michael Mattesi, whose wisdom, guidance, and unwavering belief in me have shaped my artistic journey.

Author

Michael Mattesi has authored six FORCE books, published in numerous languages, and utilized around the world to inspire and educate artists on the concept of FORCE. He has instructed FORCE Drawing for over 25 years and inspired thousands of artists.

Simultaneously, Michael has been contributing his skills as a professional artist on numerous award-winning projects in varied capacities and has collaborated with Pixar, Walt Disney Feature Animation, Walt Disney Consumer Products, Marvel Comics, Hasbro Toys, ABC, Microsoft, Electronic Arts, DreamWorks/PDI, Zynga, The School of Visual Arts, Beijing University, Art Center, Scuola Internazionale di Comics, San Jose State University, The Academy of Art University, Nickelodeon, LeapFrog, and many others. Michael's students occupy all fields of the art industry and have themselves gained prestige for their abilities.

Michael's creative and artistic, twenty five year career has provided him with a wide range of experiences across animation, video games, comics, advertising and art education. He accomplished this through a roller-coaster journey of owning a video game art resource company, shipping over 35 game titles that have won numerous awards, creating one of the earliest entertainment art schools, and writing seven books on his radical philosophy on drawing called FORCE! Michael has either worked or taught in numerous capacities from creative director to concept artist, at world class companies such as Pixar, Walt Disney Studios, Electronic Arts, Microsoft, DreamWorks/PDI, Zynga, LeapFrog and Nickelodeon and many others.

Contact him at:
Website: DrawingFORCE.com
Facebook: DrawingFORCE.com with Mike Mattesi
Instagram: michaelmattesi
Email: mike@drawingforce.com

Introduction

This book, *FORCE Fabric: How to Draw Clothes*, the seventh book in the 'FORCE' series, instructs you, the artist, how to draw clothes with FORCE.

Here we are, 20 years after I published the first FORCE book, and I feel a bit embarrassed to have taken this long to write a book about how to draw clothes. Clothing and fashion design represent intrinsic influence of the world's cultures, occupations, and personal expression! I admit I personally am not exactly fashion-forward, but I do appreciate the vast variety and impact of fashion from creative art to functional utility. My past employment as an art director in the video game industry offered me the opportunity to guide numerous character designers in their creation of fictional characters where fashion was a key component. Sure, maybe you are not into fashion, but I can guarantee you are affected by it through some form of entertainment, be it video games, live action film or television, animation or comics, and ultimately by the clothes worn by you and those around you.

Let's admit that the nude figure is the best way to learn the fundamentals of drawing. We learn how to draw from the nude model. But the end result, with most art, is presented with clothed figures. This book instructs artists to see clothing in a new, unique way, through FORCE. Clear, concise, and informal writing, coupled with my and Mritunjay's drawings of clothed models, will teach you to see FORCE in clothing. In the end, a new awareness of fabric, folds, and clothing will help you recognize important cues, use this knowledge as a tool to create form and appealing FORCE shapes, and employ clothing to support character and design in your drawings. Welcome to *FORCE Fabric*!

I put great effort into how this book is constructed and designed so you the artist can understand and use it to improve your skills! Let me explain to you how to use this book. I came to the conclusion that three main topics of discussion in drawing fashion are as follows:

1. FORCE Fundamentals: FORCE, Form and Shape

2. How Fabric Folds: Types of Fabric and Different Folds

3. Fit: Tight, medium, and loose

Let's first discuss some overarching key concepts before we enter the specifics of drawing clothes.

DOI: 10.1201/9781351049467-1

Key Concepts

THE FUNCTIONAL DESIGN OF CLOTHES

In order for me to understand a subject, I try to hover outside of it as far as I can, to not make any assumptions and imagine that this is a new subject to me. When learning about Fabric, I took nothing for granted so I'd ask myself some basic questions:

1. What role does gravity play in fabric and clothing design?
2. Why is clothing tailored and/or draped in the manners we are accustomed to?
3. What is the purpose of clothing?
4. Why are different fabrics used to construct clothes?

These bigger, broader questions lead me to answers that are also broader, hierarchical so I can dive deeper into more accurate and unassumed answers, answers with some supporting information behind them. I will attempt to answer these questions based on research and my own personal experiences.

WHAT ROLE DOES GRAVITY PLAY IN CLOTHING DESIGN? OR FASHION DESIGN?

Without gravity, our clothes and not to mention, our anatomy would be entirely different than it is now. We must always keep in mind the invisible FORCE of gravity. Our clothes hang on the frame of our body. Primarily designed around a generic standing pose, tops hang from our shoulders while pants, dresses, and skirts hang from our waist. At the waist, we need extra support to make certain the apparel does not slide down to our feet so we use belts and elastic bands to do the job. Fashion designers give attention to the weight of a fabric and how it folds and drapes due to the body and gravity.

WHY IS CLOTHING TAILORED AND/OR DRAPED THE WAY IT IS?

Gravity is a key factor in clothing design. Clothes hang on the anatomical structure of the body and must allow us to move and function during our everyday tasks. So, from the utilitarian side of this discussion, clothes stay attached or hang off of our bodies, responding to gravity and the movements of the human body.

WHAT IS THE PURPOSE OF CLOTHING?

This answer to this question invokes a much broader conversation. We could make quite a long list describing the numerous purposes of clothes. To name a few, there are privacy, self-expression, corporate and sports branding, uniformity to an organization, job responsibility, and political and group allegiances. Take into consideration time periods, raw materials, and climates, and we multiply these answers almost infinitely.

DOI: 10.1201/9781351049467-2

WHY ARE DIFFERENT FABRICS USED TO CONSTRUCT CLOTHES?

Fabric can define emotion and story of an outfit. Fabric defines how the outfit will fall and fold on the body. For example, will the folds be long, elegant swooping lines or stiff and angular? Does the fabric disguise the forms of the figure underneath or embellish areas of the human body? Perhaps the fabric contains a pattern that defines an artist or time period. It can represent a certain culture of the world. I guess we can say the different fabrics present us with endless opportunities for communication and expression.

HOW IS THIS "HOW TO DRAW CLOTHES" BOOK DIFFERENT FROM OTHERS?

There are other books that teach the subject of drawing clothing. With this book, I am going to share with you an understanding of WHY clothes function the way they do and HOW this happens in relation to FORCE and the human body. When you are done learning the material in this book and practicing it, you will draw clothes from reference or your imagination that truly function the way they do in reality. This in turn will bring a more satisfying believability to your work.

Although we learn to draw from the human figure, typically the nude human figure, most art depicts people that are clothed. The clothes worn, whether in the real world or an imaginative one, represent a character. Each article of clothing worn is a decision, and each decision says something specific about its wearer.

When used correctly, clothing makes drawing the figure not only enjoyable but simpler than drawing the nude. It -is rare to draw an outfit or costume more complex than the anatomy of the human body.

I must mention that starting with clothing without an understanding of the human form, can be confusing and complex. These feelings are typically due to a lack of understanding about the function of the figure, and its balance created by rhythm relative to gravity. My experience drawing the figure has taught me that hierarchical thinking gives me a more well-rounded understanding of the subject I am drawing. Learn to draw the figure first, after all, there are no outfits without a figure to hang them on, a foundation. I Recommend my *FORCE: Dynamic Life Drawing* and *FORCE: Anatomy Books* to learn more on this subject. If you have my other FORCE books, you know that great drawing skills come from seeing clearly, understanding your subject, and the physical skill of mark making. You'll once again need all three to best learn how to draw fabric that creates clothes.

HOW FABRIC IS CREATED

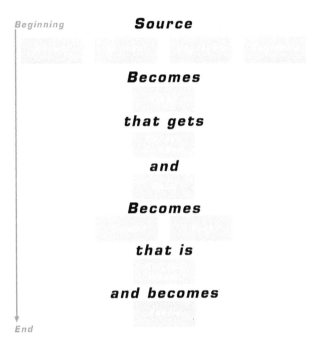

Beginning

Source

Becomes

that gets

and

Becomes

that is

and becomes

End

The flow chart above is rudimentary and does not cover every option on the journey from source material to fabric, but instead gives you a general overview to better understand fabric creation. Fabric starts at mainly four source materials: animal, vegetable, mineral, and synthetic. All of these materials go through a felting process in order to be turned into fibers. These fibers are then either carded or combed. This process converts the fibers into threads through spinning the fibers, and this spinning creates threads. The threads and/or yarn are woven in a number of different ways and then become a specific fabric. Fabric gets cut into different shapes known as flats and finally sewn together to create clothing.

HUMANITY AND AWE

I have taught and lectured in many schools around the world and the one element I see missing in art instruction is humanity. Almost all art instruction with a figure model is used to learn how to draw through measuring instead of experiencing the richness of humanity. Once you have a bigger purpose to draw than learning how to draw, what I sometimes call a carrot, you will learn faster. You will be more eager to understand FORCE, perspective, anatomy, and everything else that goes into becoming a great draftsperson!

When drawing the model, stay present and in utter awe! When the model takes the stand, it is as if they are a god or goddess presented to us. They represent you and the rest of humanity. Become amazed and stay open to this fantastic occurrence. Your experience with the model is your drawing. Therefore, the more rich, incredible, and dramatic your experience, the more rich, incredible, and dramatic your drawing. You are the vehicle to this journey so if you are closed and fearful, so is your work. Use the idea of having the richest and most stimulating experience drawing the model's humanity while using your very own as the purpose to drawing. All of the technique throughout the rest of this book is to serve that higher purpose.

What is there to be in awe of? Look at the amount of effort the model gives you. A living, breathing person is in front of you. Notice their lungs fill with oxygen and how they present you with stress, tension, and torque. Look at their muscles and bones perform great moments. Each particular person chooses particular poses. Be sensitive to that. Are the poses poetic, athletic, romantic, relaxed, masculine, or feminine? What stories does your humanity find in their poses? You must be sensitive to drama! There is the drama of the pose, the drama of FORCE, the drama of structure, the drama of depth, the drama of shape, and the drama of texture. As you can see, there is plenty of drama to be in awe of.

TRUTH

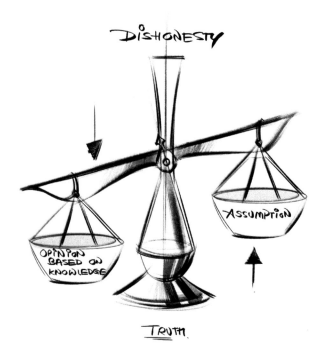

This illustration shows that the increase of opinion based on knowledge brings us closer to the truth and further from dishonesty. You need to gain knowledge to comprehend what to have an opinion about and to obtain the capacity to actualize the opinions you possess upon the page. In this way, your opinion will bring you closer to the model's reality. Every line presents an opinion.

Two ways of clarifying your opinions are through exaggeration and analogy. Using analogies helps you form opinions. 'His leg is like a column of strength; the FORCES are like a roller coaster.' I use many analogies throughout this book to make myself clear to you. If you have something to say, learn how to express it as best you can. Students tell me they are afraid to exaggerate because it is not real. You have a much greater opportunity to capture reality through what you conceive as an exaggeration of ideas than you do working on a dead representation of life via copying. Copying leads to lying.

Push what the model gives you. Go after the functional and poetic ideas. If a pose is about torque, then draw and experience torque. If it is about relaxation, then make it clearly about relaxation. State clearly what you have to say. I love loud drawings, not whispers.

The work of art is the exaggeration of the idea.

Andre' Gide

Glen Keane is one of today's leading artists when it comes to exaggerating the clarity of a moment. He is extraordinary at imbuing his animation drawings with heart. If a character is powerful, you feel their power; if sad, you feel their sadness. His drawings are always loud and opinionated. If you don't know who he is, go see his performances of the main characters in films like The Little Mermaid, Beauty and the Beast, Aladdin, Pocahontas, Tarzan, and Treasure Planet, to name a few.

IN THE ZONE, FLOW, PRESENCE

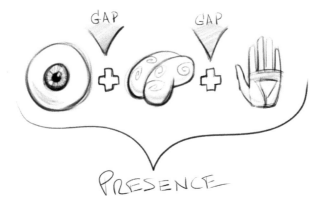

During the act of drawing, we move through three steps: seeing, thinking about what we see, and then using our hand to draw it. The issues that occur with this process are in the gaps between the steps. Typically, we look at something and then our minds create their own version of what we saw, an assumption. Then we draw THAT idea, our mind's idea. Closing this first gap between the eye and the mind is crucial. Your mind needs to believe what it actually sees. Try drawing without looking at the page. Then to close the second gap, focus on your hand moving at the speed your eye sees and your mind thinks. So become a FORCE drawing addict and feel the power of drawing in FLOW, in the moment!

A current, popular discussion in our world is the concept of flow which is the state you get into where all focus is on the task at hand, where time either speeds up or slows down and your mind is like a laser. This same idea has existed for centuries within Buddhism. The act of drawing is a perfect vehicle for experiencing flow. In fact, in my twenty plus years of teaching, I have always said that this state is the goal we are after, and once reached, it is like an addiction. I just found out that science proves that many of the body's natural 'feel good' chemicals are released into the body when in a state of flow.

PASSION

You must be passionate and driven to learn and be great. Love it, hate it, and have an emotional experience. Always push yourself to new levels and enjoy the trip. No one strives for mediocrity. Give the drawing everything you've got in the limited amount of time you have with the model. This is the fundamental FORCE behind a student's progression. How can you or an instructor critique your work if it is not your full effort? The critique is then based on only a percent of your ability. You have to believe that you can obtain the goals you are after. In terms of myself, everything I have achieved is due to knowing clearly what I wanted, I intensely wanted it, and some part of me knew I could get it.

FEAR

You are probably wondering how fear would have anything to do with drawing, but it has everything to do with it. Fear kills passion. Fear is the most detrimental attribute a student could have. The greatest fear is the fear of failing which in this case is creating a 'bad' drawing. Remember, if you are drawing in order to capture the humanity of the model, you will become unconcerned about your drawing. Be aware of your experience and just stay present with the model. There is no failing, only results. Be courageous and push yourself to new heights. Besides, what is going to happen if you make a 'bad' decision? You will learn from it. The more results you create, the faster you will reach your destination. It is not as if we are skydiving. You will always land safely, no matter how great the risks. Consider yourself the ultimate stunt person.

INTERNAL DIALOG

Use it to help you, not hurt you. Stay aware of what you say to yourself, in your mind. Notice when and why you are indecisive or concerned. Brain wash yourself if need be. 'I know exactly what I am doing….' In time, a statement like this becomes a reality. As you learn about FORCE, you will come to realize that your mind will be occupied thinking about numerous ideas and that means there will be no time for you to judge yourself. Your mindset is essential to this dialogue. Stay curious and hungry to learn. Experience the ten thousand hours of drawing and learning that give you the sense of accomplishment that comes with practice!

ITERATION

The fastest way to learn is to fail early and fail fast. As an artist, you do this by focusing on the big ideas and drawing them quickly with some fervor. Quick drawings or sketches give you the opportunity to draw a pose and outfit over and over again before you commit to the best option. In fact, iteration gives a quick progression of improvement and choices. You also learn to not commit too early and to not be too precious with your drawings.

RISK

In order to grow, you must take risk, or what you perceive as risk. Risk to one individual is the norm to another. Be aware of that. Use your curiosity and passion for learning to push through your risks. This is where your courage and pride will come from. In order to have opinion, you MUST be able to take risk! You MUST move beyond.

OPINION

Strengthening your ability to take greater and greater risks allows you to get out of the 'kind of' mindset. New students look at life and 'kind of' see it. You must see truth in order to form opinion. Opinions come from heightened clarity! Much of this clarity comes from knowledge. Your search for knowledge comes from curiosity. Don't draw with mediocrity, stride for opinion through clarity. What are you trying to say? How do you feel during your experience of drawing the subject? The act of drawing many hours alone without some real thought might get you some muscle memory but you must observe yourself and your work to improve upon both.

Use creative ideas when drawing FORCE. You might have a thought that is an analogy. Perhaps the figure's pose reminds you of a natural power, architecture, culture, a time period, a character, automobile, or other famous artist's work. Draw upon your intuition to inspire your experience.

THE POWER OF QUESTIONS

When you stare at the white paper and then back at the model and start thinking, 'I don't know what to do!' it is time to control your thoughts and shift your focus to the power of questions. The question that got me out of doubt and turmoil is 'What do I want?' This very powerful question forces your mind into creating answers. 'I want to find the largest FORCE and experience it! I want to see shape and design in the figure. I want to learn how to draw FORCE!'

ENVISION AND EMPOWERMENT

When I was in art school, I would play games with my mind. I would look at the model and then envision my drawing on the page. My image of my drawing was far beyond my abilities at that time but I do believe that the repetition of this activity allowed me to believe in myself and attain my goals more quickly. It is empowering to ask yourself if you are doing your best and answering honestly. You are capable of more than you are achieving. Hold yourself to excellence. I promise you that you will be amazed by your true potential!!!

When you look down at your drawing and it is not what you envisioned, that is great! Notice the differences between the envisioned and the reality. Now you know what you need to work on and you can set goals to go after! It may be that you notice your drawing does not have enough form and anatomy and that is why you are reading this book!

CONTRAST AND AFFINITY

While working at Walt Disney Feature Animation, one of the best rules I learned was 'CONTRAST CREATES INTEREST.' Beware mediocrity through the lack of contrast. Look for idiosyncrasies, asymmetry, unparalleled moments, and varied line. This rule works for character design, landscape painting, film editing, writing, and all works artistic. Contrast is self-explanatory but how many ideas can be contrasted? That is where the magic happens. A line on a piece of paper can have much contrast or little contrast. Is the line parallel to the edges of the paper or is it at a 45 degree angle? Is there variety in the weight of the line? How long or short is the line? Does it go off of the page? When drawing the human figure, we think we all look alike … we all have two arms, legs, eyes, etc. The real magic happens when you see the idiosyncratic nuances. 'Wow, this model's elbows are larger than mine, her hip is long and thin, he has a heavy brow.'

All of these possibilities represent different ideas in the world of art. Remember that every mark on the page has meaning, a meaning to create the bigger purpose of the artist's statement!

Affinity or unity means the similarity between items in the drawings. This gives you another opportunity for contrast … the contrast between contrast and affinity.

Design is an abstract way of looking at our world and using it to communicate our thoughts. Your art is only as powerful as your thoughts and how you communicate them with your skills. I hope to present you with some new tools to assist you in communicating your experiences.

Were the diver to think on the jaws of the shark he would never lay hands on the precious pearl.

Sa'di Gulistan

LEARNING PROCESS

Art does not reproduce the visible; rather, it makes visible.

Paul Klee

Students who open themselves up to learning are the ones that move ahead quickly. Take what you understand and agree with and use it to further yourself. Some students will actually argue their habits or limitations.

Argue for your limitations, and sure enough, they're yours.

Richard Bach

These students move nowhere in their minds for sometimes a month, a semester, or even a whole year. Don't waste your time with bad habits! Seek to understand! If you keep doing what you know at present, you will keep getting the same results.

Before starting on the journey ahead, I want to share with you some of my key concepts.

IMPORTANCE OF THE NUDE MODEL

The optimal way to learn how to draw clothes is to learn how to draw the nude figure first. The knowledge acquired through this experience will allow you to draw more believable clothing. Since this is a FORCE drawing book, we know how important it is to comprehend the FORCES of the body. These FORCES play a huge roll in the folds of fabric in clothing.

The other major component in drawing clothes is our second FORCE, gravity. The constant perfectly vertical downward FORCE of gravity pulls fabric on the body and is a big detriment in the actual design of our clothes. Let's look at the chart below and see how these two major FORCE categories work relative to one another.

HIERARCHY

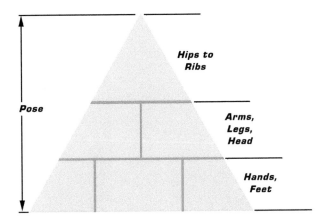

The shape of a pyramid gives us an icon of hierarchy or an order of importance. In the beginning, draw and think with the most important or core idea first; details come last. The pyramid is the human body and the story its posture implies. The top of this pyramid shows the number one concept. This portrays your first representation of the model. This will be the main idea, or FORCE, of what the model is doing. For instance, standing straight, bending over, seated, etc. Think from large to small. You always want to go after the main idea first. The bottom of the pyramid would be fingernails or something equally insignificant. Don't get caught up in the small things until you first know the main idea.

Animation is also a hierarchical process. Here the entire pyramid symbolizes the character's actions instead of one drawing's forces. The animator's drawings are represented by the pyramid's peak. He draws the key moments of a character's actions. The team of inbetweeners, the rest of the pyramid that works with him, then further develops these motions. Their drawings go in between the key drawings the animator created.

An illustrator or concept artist must be aware of the story or main point of the image. Then, progressive decisions are made that support that idea from layout to grayscale, color, and effects.

ARTISTS AND MODEL REFERENCE

Mritunjay Varun, official FORCE instructor, and myself, Michael Mattesi, are the illustrators for this FORCE book. Since Mritunjay is the primary illustrator, any drawing by me will be labeled "By Michael Mattesi". Many hours of drawing, editing, and redrawing have gone into the great passion, curiosity, and skill found in the drawings. Family members, including myself and my daughters Marin and Makenna, modeled. You'll find my brother in law, Chris, among the pages and models from Argentina, Trinda and Noe, along with our models from India, Devashish Puri and Priya Sharma.

SUPPLIES

Students in my in-person classes/workshops draw on a 18"×24" smooth newsprint. Students draw with very soft, graphite crayons or wax tools such as black China marker or Caran D'Ache. I don't want drawing class to focus on fancy mediums. Everyone uses the same supplies. These supplies have been chosen over years of instructing. Smooth Newsprint is cheap and the smooth paper with wax or really soft graphite is a slick and smooth drawing experience. Digital drawing is typically accomplished in Adobe Photoshop, Clip Studio Paint on a Wacom Cintiqu or on the iPad in ProCreate.

Gravity as Designer

FORCE Fabric starts with gravity! Yes, why are our clothes designed the way they are? Well, it is first about gravity, and then it is about the function and frame of our anatomy. Since there is a constant FORCE pulling down on everything, clothing needs to hang on our frames. The human figure is anatomically designed to work with the Gravity FORCE. In order to draw clothing on a figure, you must first learn how to draw the figure with FORCE. I suggest reading the book *FORCE: Dynamic Life Drawing* to better understand this drawing approach for drawing the human figure. This knowledge will help you better understand the concepts presented in this book relative to clothes. All of the model drawings in this book will be illustrated with the FORCE drawing approach from the prior-mentioned book.

DOI: 10.1201/9781351049467-3

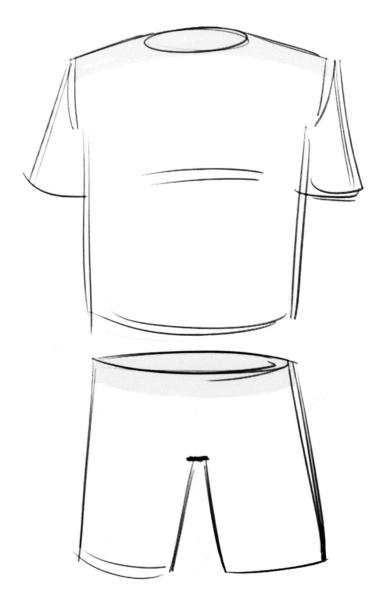

Observing a simple shirt and a pair of shorts, we can see the green Gravity FORCE regions that are most strongly affected by the Gravity FORCE. The shirt hangs off of the top of the shoulder area. The vast majority of tops we wear work with this same function, hanging off the shoulder. Then, we put a hole in the top for our neck and head, a perfect way for us to hide and protect our upper body.

In the drawing of shorts, there is nothing to hang on top of as we did with the shirt. We see how we designed clothes to instead hug the waistline. The heavier the shorts, pants, skirt, etc., the more need arises for a belt or elastic band, some kind of support.

Think about the invention of suspenders that suspended or hung the pants off of the shoulders!

FORCE FUNDAMENTALS

We need to understand the function and FORCES of the figure beneath the fabric because this function represents one of the two FORCES the fabric is responding to. The FORCE of the body and the FORCE of gravity are always active and must be considered when drawing the fabric of clothing.

The FORCE Line

In order to draw with FORCE, we want to speak with the language of the FORCE line. Let's first look at common line types from artists.

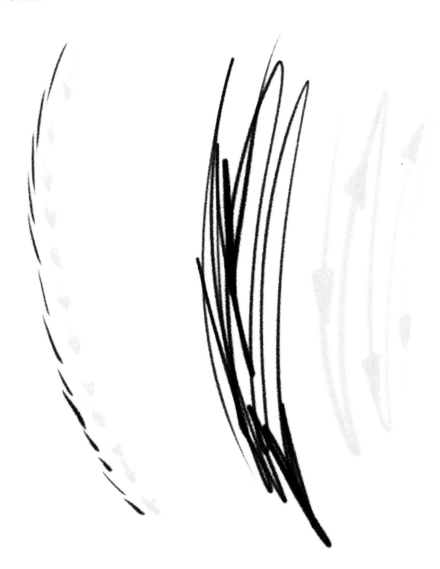

Left: This is the infamous hairy line. Uncertainty and fear take us across the page through thousands of broken thoughts instead of drawing one line per idea. Drawing like this never gives you the opportunity to move on to bigger ideas or feel FORCE and direction in your hand and mind.

Right: It is sketchy and created by backward and forward motions. No direction. The line or, more importantly, its idea does not start somewhere, have a purpose, and go somewhere. There is no clear idea.

So, that leads us to our FORCE line. The core idea is that the line actually represents the idea of FORCE! One line = one Directional FORCE = one idea. The line starts somewhere, does something, and goes somewhere. This is achieved with a confident stroking of the paper with the pencil. The arrow example shows you the direction of the energy or its path. This is Directional FORCE.

Forewarning: I am not suggesting uptightness with the line. You don't have to get it right the first time. Let your hand sweep over the paper's surface in the directions that the model moves in until you have absorbed the pose's idea. Then make your marks by slowly applying pressure to the paper with the pencil while you are still in motion. Notice how you can control the line's value. This discipline of mark making is of tremendous value because when you draw, your head will already think about where energy comes from, what it is doing, and where it goes. Feel liberated and excited, and be courageous.

Throughout the book, I will use the color BLUE to present Directional and Tension FORCES.

When drawing the nude figure, there exists Directional FORCES and when drawing clothing we can also think about Tension FORCES. Depending on the fit of the clothing, such as tight fit to loose fit, the clothing is more or less affected by the FORCES of the figure itself. Because of this truth, I am introducing TENSION FORCE. The above image shows the ability of these two types of FORCES to act contradictory to one another. The above rhythm of the figure directs FORCE from the back to the stomach and the tension in the shirt move from the armpit to the back of the pelvis. Our skin is like a tight outfit and thus acts like tight-fitting clothes. At other times, the two moments can be different because more loose fabric may also be responding to gravity instead of the FORCES of the figure.

APPLIED FORCE

Besides the Directional FORCE line giving us a linear direction or path of FORCE, it also informs us how much FORCE is applied upon it. This Applied FORCE represents the body and the direction it moves as a mass.

If lines were roads, you would obviously be able to drive your car through a straightaway faster than you would through a curve. The tighter a curve, the more FORCE you would feel expended since you changed the initial trajectory of that FORCE. When driving through the curve, the place where you would feel the most amount of FORCE would be at its apex. The FORCE would diminish as you pulled out of it, allowing you to regain speed.

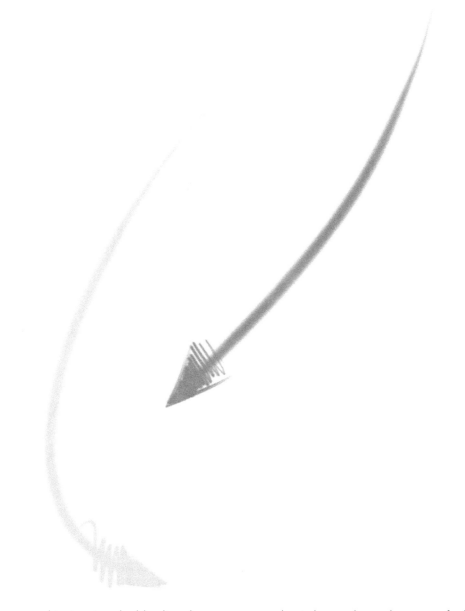

If we add gravity to this situation, the blue line shows us a mass that is bottom heavy because of where the apex of the curve is located on the line. The direction of the mass is defined by its apex, which was defined by the orange Applied FORCE. If we look at both of the arrows, we get a sense of their connected relationship.

In these three images, notice how the differing apexes suggest different directions of Applied FORCE relative to the Blue Directional FORCES. The center illustration has the least amount of Applied FORCE since it is so close to straight. The image on the right shows a strong Applied FORCE pushing high up on the Directional FORCE curve. The orange shapes represent the body's mass, the Blue Directional lines, and a contour of the figure.

When you drive a car on a straight piece of road, it deals with gravity, pulling the car down into the ground and there is friction, caused by gravity, which determines the weight of the car. What happens if the car hits a curve at the speed it traveled on the straight road? At the apex of the curve, we will experience the most amount of inertial change. This concept is important as we learn to draw the fabrics of clothing.

Let's start with a real clear example of Applied FORCE as we can see the weight of the bag pulled down by gravity causing whatever material with to push down on the inside of the bag. The FORCE on the upper back driven down by the bag's weight, squeezes its way out from under this weight, counterbalances in the pelvis in the figure creating what I call and S torso.

Look at the long, beautiful rhythms and how they connect the full system of the figure from head to toe. Understanding these FORCE flows will dramatically help you understand how fabric is affecting by these energies and their directions. Try to imagine the folds in the fabrics as the model bends as twists over her right hip.

The C torso here will cause fabric to stretch on the right side of the body and fold up on the left. The parted legs will define stretch in the fabric from the cotch and compress around the outside edge of the knee.

As the leg is squashed by the weight of the figure, we all know that many folds will occur behind the knee because densely compressed material will be trapped there. We also can surmise that there would be stretched or hanging fabric along the page left side of the drawing, along the ribcage since the arm is lifted. Depending on how tight the model's shirt is, we may even see the S curve move across the torso.

The strong, straight leg will allow for fabric to hang from the hip if the clothing fit is loose or medium. Since the other leg is on an angle, the fabric will hang from the front of the back of the leg and off of the front. Lastly, the extended arm will act as a curtain rod for loose fabric as it slides to the wrist and hangs from the arm.

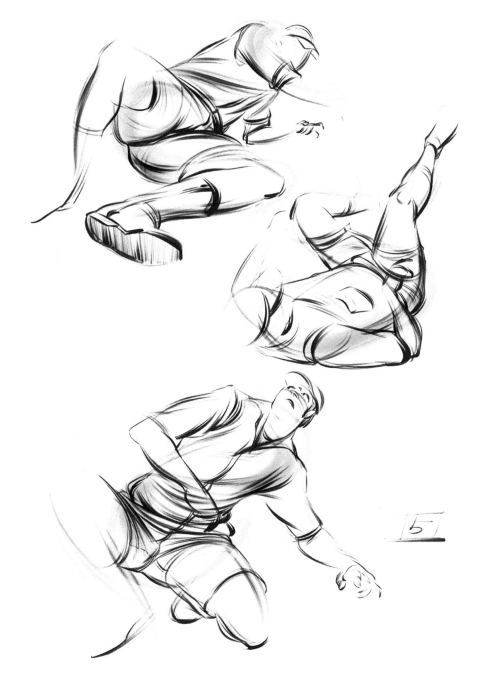

In this fun series, we added more fabric and more clothing. Look at the correlation between the Directional FORCES of the poses and the Tension FORCES found in the folds of the fabric. On the body, I call the blue lines Directional FORCE, and for the clothing, we can call the blue lines Tension FORCES. In the top drawing, see the S torso move Directional FORCE from the upper torso diagonally across the mid-section to the opposite side of the body to the top areas of the pelvis. The Blue Directional FORCE path presents this rhythm. Now look at the folds in the shirt and see how they too pull across the front of the torso in this S like path presenting the rhythm of the figure underneath the shirt. The folds do the same as the figure giving us clear S curve Tension FORCE.

Let's get more complicated with the clothing and the poses. Notice the S rhythmic moment of Tension FORCE presented across the right leg that moves from the back of the pelvis, around the thigh and then to the front and top of the knee. At the right shoulder, we see a great deal of Applied FORCE that pulls the fabric across the back from the waist line. Once we reach the shoulder, the Tension FORCE and fabric fall toward the forearm.

This unique outfit shows us what I call a C torso that sweeps over the back and pushes into the left shoulder.
Then, we move through an outside, inside outside leg template built around Directional FORCES that rhythmically
shoot down the right leg. The tank on the back and its pelvic harness helps clearly present the center of the torso.
Folds found in this leg don't show much tension versus compression that helps define form.

In our final drawing for this section, try to see for yourself how the Directional FORCES of the figure help generate the Tension FORCES found in the folds of the clothes. Above, you can see a quick, shape driven gesture drawing thumbnail to help capture the gestalt of the pose.

This series of drawings, where I am modeling, shows how an action of the body can affect the Tension FORCES of the Navy Pea Coat's fabric due to Directional, Applied, and Gravitational FORCES. Remember that blue on clothing is Tension FORCE and Orange is Applied FORCES. The floating Blue arrows are Directional FORCES. Gravity allows this heavy Navy Peacoat to rise only a certain amount based on its weight relative to my body's rotational FORCE. Here, we can see how the Tension FORCES are strongly influenced by the Directional FORCES indicating the torque FORCE.

This second series show my body rotating and tilting at the same time, thrusting my right shoulder's Directional FORCE forward and downward. This action lifts the tail of the coat at the end of the action and causes many folds to occur in the coat's overlapping action. Clothing has the ability to enhance the Directional and Applied FORCES of the body's actions.

THE FABRIC SPEEDOMETER

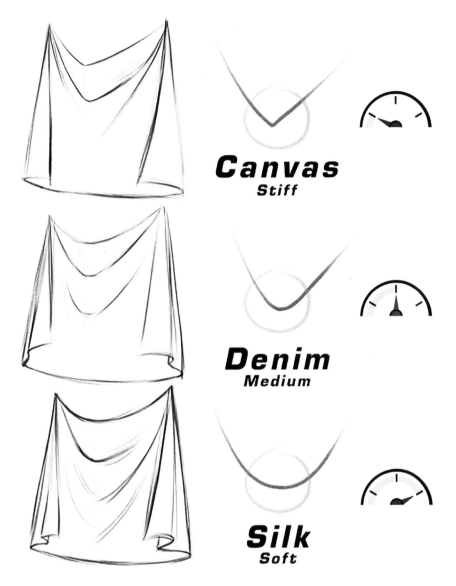

What good is a FORCE Clothing Book without a speedometer to tell you the speed that a particular fabric conveys? Each fabric has an innate sense of softness or hardness, and this determines how open (obtuse) or tight (acute) the curves of the fold bends can become.

In the drawing above, we have our three fabrics showing us a U fold. Notice that the break created in each is due to gravity and the firmness of the fabric. We can think of the type of break presenting a different speed. Firm or stiff fabric folds are like canvas where a softer fabric such as silk, is more pliable and creates wider curves, more graceful folds.

Think about line presenting speed. That means when you have a more open or obtuse fold in fabric, the speed of that fabric is faster and when the fold is compressed and has an acute radius, it is a much slower curve or fold. You would have to drive more slowly though an acute curve versus an obtuse fold. The speedometers above will show up later when we analyze different folds and fits of clothing.

ANCHOR POINTS

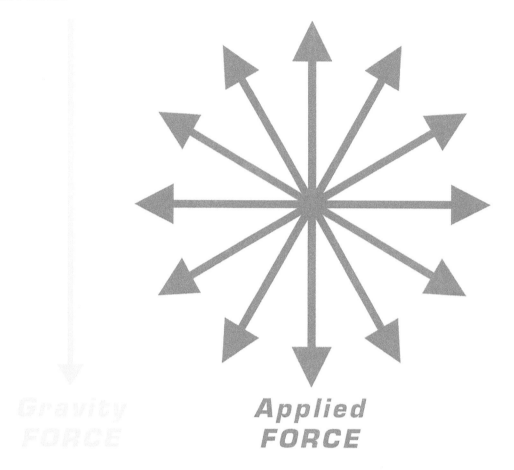

Gravity FORCE

Applied FORCE

GRAVITATIONAL ANCHOR POINT

There are two types of anchor points, Gravity and Applied FORCE. Anchor points play a major role in how fabric functions and folds relative to the body. The first way they work is through Gravity FORCE. Gravity is why, at a fundamental level, our clothes are built the way they are. Our clothes hang on the body's frame. At the top of our physique, we find our shoulders and top of our ribcage where our head and neck poke out of clothing. So our shirts, coats, jackets, etc. either have a hole on top for our heads and necks or wrap around the neck to hang over our shoulders. Draping a scarf over the shoulders or around the neck is a great example of the use of a fabric working with our anatomy and just hanging.

APPLIED FORCE ANCHOR POINT

The second anchor point is caused by Applied FORCE! The anchor point occurs when the body's FORCES cause the point, not gravity. Any time we move our bodies away from an upright, straight, and standing position, a zero pose, we use Applied FORCE, and those FORCES cause Applied FORCE Anchor Points. Tension FORCE is what occurs along the fabric between two anchor points or an anchor point and the hanging edge of fabric such as the bottom of a skirt.

Welcome to Freddie, our FORCE Fabric, currently unaffected by gravity and by the FORCES of the figure. He floats in a vacuum with no external energy to affect him.

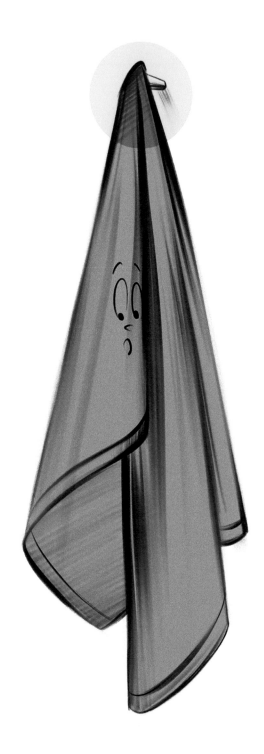

The first FORCE that affects Freddie is Gravity, just allowing him to hang. This concept is what apparel is designed around, the idea to hang on the frames of our bodies. We can trust the FORCE of gravity.

The second main FORCE that affects Freddie, our FORCE Fabric, is Applied FORCE. This FORCE occurs where the body is pushing against fabric and thus generates folds. Above we can see the fabric poked upward and to the right, causing folds downward and to the left due to this pull. This action of the body causes an Applied FORCE Anchor Point.

This fold hangs from a Gravity Anchor Point and wraps around this tube, which will become anatomy when we bring these concepts to the figure. Around the back of the tube could exist either a Gravity Anchor Point that point is purely hanging or an Applied FORCE Anchor Point if the tube is rotating and therefore actively pulling the fabric.

The one instance where Freddie is most dissatisfied is when there are no anchor points. He sits inert, crumpled on the ground. There is nothing for him to hang from and nothing pulling him in a direction. This is important to understand. If you become aware of Gravity and Applied FORCE Anchor Points, then understanding fold types created by these concepts becomes much easier to comprehend, observe, and bring to your own illustrations!

First let's look at some drawings, analyzing how these two different anchor points present their importance to comprehension of the ideas.

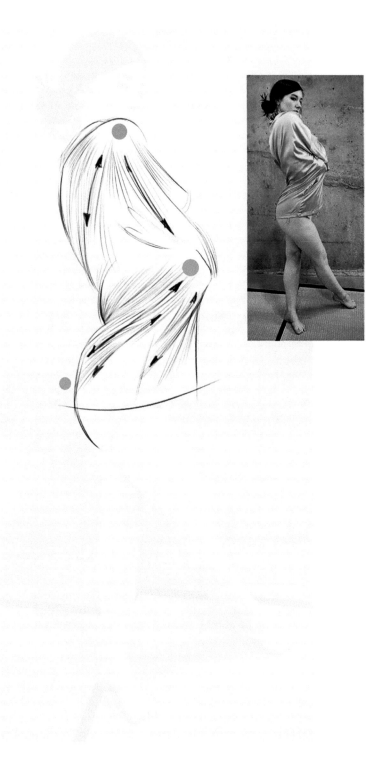

This is a good time to use a clothed model photo. Marie stands here in a silk robe. The image shares with us clear folds due to three Applied FORCE Anchor Points. Draw the folds with lots of FORCE Tension lines to more clearly define the relationship between the points and the folds. In time, you will learn to edit and pick the folds you most need to describe the clothing.

One more image of Marie shows us two Gravity and one Applied FORCE Anchor Points. The multiple FORCE Tension lines exhibit the tension of the folds caused by these anchor points.

Gravity Anchor Points are a great start for understanding how to draw folds. Gravity plays its quintessential roll here presenting how it consistently pulls fabric downward with its FORCE. See how the model's hands create two Gravitational Anchor Points from which the fabric hangs. Most Tension FORCE occurs at the hands and then where the most Applied FORCE would be found, at the base of the curve of the folds.

As you can see, this pose contains a loose-fitting shirt that shows how it responds to Gravity and Applied FORCE. The green, Gravity Anchor Point in the shoulder, and the orange, Applied FORCE Anchor Point at the elbow, pull the fabric with great Tension FORCE while the wrist rotates it. Notice the varying Tension FORCES between these points and their directions. Many of the folds help create the form of the upper and lower arms as well. We want to edit folds when possible. Use what you need and discard the rest.

In this illustration on Anchor Points, it is not the FORCE of gravity causing Tension FORCE but instead the Applied FORCES of the model's body. See the Tension FORCE point at the raised elbow that pulls on the fabric across the back of the arm. Below, the second hand grabs the fabric and tugs it to the left, stretching fabric across the center of the torso.

The model is actively pulling on the fabric from two Applied FORCE Anchor Points causing aggressive Tension FORCES from one hand to the other. Also notice the Gravity Anchor Points found at the shoulders where the fabric hangs downward and pulls into the lower hands' anchor points, an interesting combination of the Gravity and Applied FORCE Anchor Points caused by those two FORCES. Lots of Tension FORCE is generated between the anchor points.

01

02

03

I started my career at Walt Disney Feature Animation which inspired me to view the world through physics and FORCES. In animation, we attempt to create clear efficiency in the work on all levels of artistry and clothing is no exception. Above I have removed the majority of folds to simplify and thus clarify the ideas of the pose. Sometimes, folds could be left over from a prior moment of the body that does not pertain to the one you are drawing. Understanding the different anchor points helps us understand how to simplify.

ASSIGNMENTS

1. Practice drawing the FORCE line.

2. Build confidence.

3. Use FORCE Experience exercises, A to B Line, Circles and Ellipses, Skating, Roller Coaster, to keep improving FORCE Line.

4. Bring these experiences and improved line to the figure. Find single areas of Directional FORCE in the figure and draw them.

5. Try connecting the Directional FORCES with Applied FORCES to create rhythms.

6. Stay aware of gravity when drawing the figure to better understand how the body works.

7. Find photos of models and draw on top of them identifying Gravity and Applied FORCE Anchor Points. Draw Tension FORCE lines in-between those points to describe the tension found there.

This book is about drawing fabric so not all of the above subjects are taught in this book. You can find them on DrawingFORCE.com or in the FORCE: Dynamic Life Drawing Book.

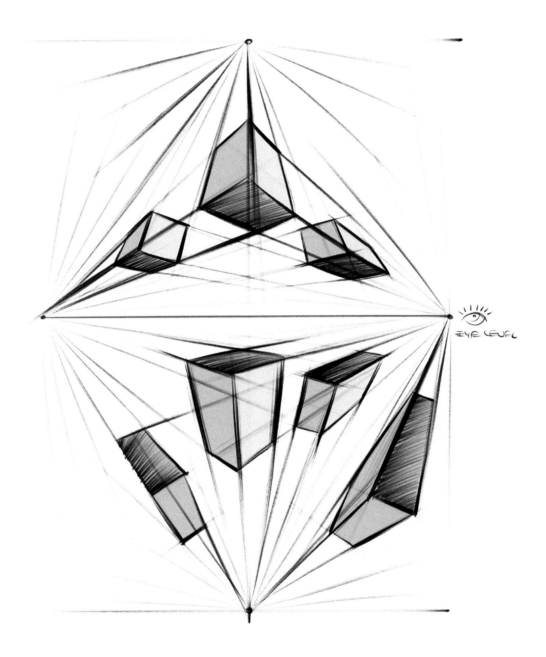

EYE LEVEL

You must learn the perspective grid in order to draw well. Comprehending how the anchor of the horizon line connects vanishing points that then control the outward fanning of extension lines is crucial to good drawing. The angles made by the extension lines, and how they cross each other emanating from one vanishing point to another, define the way we perceive three-dimensional space on the two-dimensional plane of the page or screen. Ingenious.

THREE-DIMENSIONAL SPACE AND VOLUME

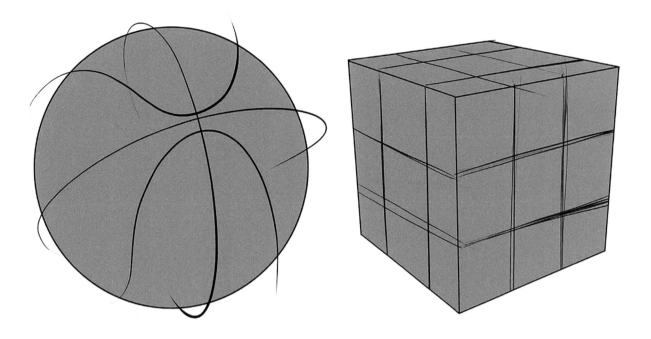

The capacity to successfully draw form and depth comes from and understanding of the perspective grid. Training with a four-point grid that evolves to a freehand box and primitives' rotations allows us to understand figures in absolute space and then their forms within relative space. When it comes to clothing, form is most clearly represented in the clothing structure, such as seams, collars, cuffs, waistlines, and hems.

First, we start with the box which we have learned to draw because of our practice within the grid. All of that practice allows us to see the correct angles that create the box without the extension lines. This is relative space.

A plane of a box gives us the proportions and angles we need to successfully draw an ellipse. Once we can draw one ellipse, we can draw many subdividing the box. This leads us to drawing other primitives, simple geometric forms, that need the ellipse in order to be drawn well.

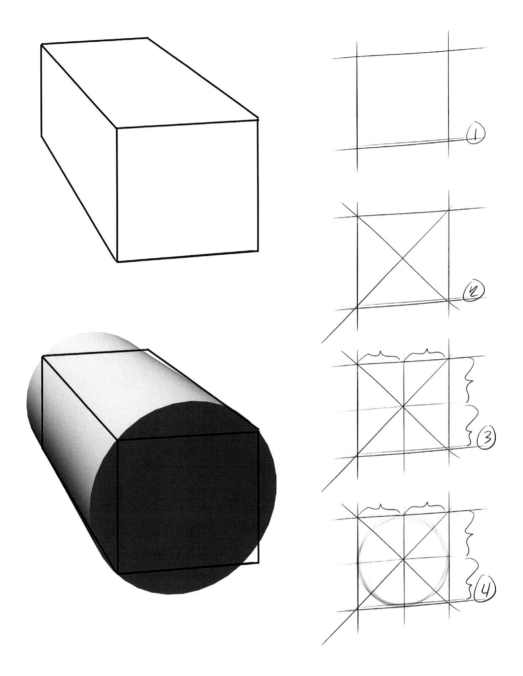

If we know how to draw the ellipse and we can draw a box in perspective, we can now draw the tube, an important primitive to drawing the human figure since arms and legs can quickly be built from this form. I find it more accurate to start with the long box since the ellipse is generated from the four planes of the box. On the right side is a step-by-step process to illustrate for you how to use a plane in perspective and subdivide it to draw an ellipse.

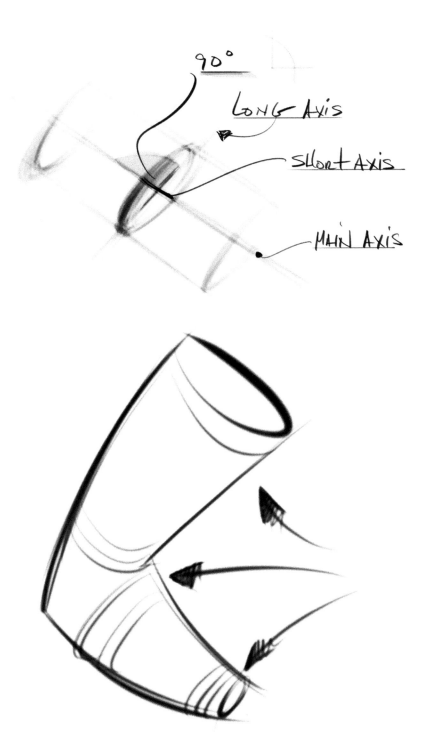

The above drawing shows an ellipse and its long and short axes. The long axis must be ninety degrees to the main axis of the object you are drawing. This makes certain the long axis of the ellipse is drawn on the correct angle relative to the object whose form you are describing. The short axis defines the angle of how open or closed the ellipse is. That describes to what degree the object is pointing toward you are is perpendicular to your eye. With some time, you will learn to create the figure efficiently with great shape and a few simple ellipses or wrapping lines that present the correct orientation of the forms in space. Here, we can see two forms that could be the upper and lower arm or a bent leg.

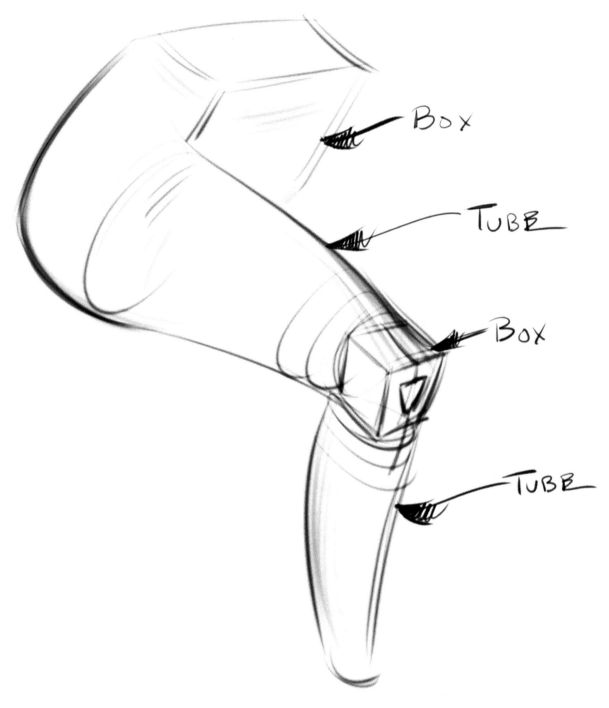

BOX

TUBE

BOX

TUBE

We want to get to a place of understanding that combines many different types of primitives of different proportions and directions in space. Above we can see how certain areas of bone and muscle can be drawn with simple tubes and the bonier joints of the body are best expressed with more of a box structure. This is shown in the knee and pelvis.

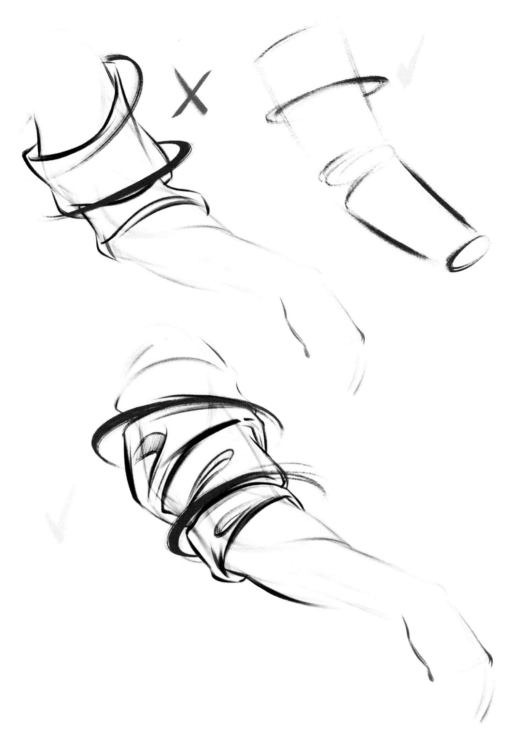

As we move into drawing fabric, we can use it to clearly present form. The drawing at the top shows folds that curve in the opposite orientation of the arm's form. In the top right corner, I drew the tubes of the arm which then makes it more clear for us to illustrate the folds with ellipses that curve the correct way to show accurate forms in space. You can see the angle of the long axis at the far ends of the ellipse and the short axis measures the width of the ellipse.

The openings found within the outfit above present clear ellipses around major forms in the figure. We can see a purple ellipse around the waist, the right arm, and the neck. Each of these ellipses is an opportunity to show form while drawing the actual objects or clothing of the figure.

Ellipses abound throughout this rhythmic pose clearly presenting how the vertical column of the different structures move into and out of the flat 2D plane of the image. This most clearly can be seen in the orientation change found at the lower back where we travel downward into the page at the bottom of the ribs and then out of the page, toward us, at the waistline of the model's shorts.

Observe all the different forms of the body shown with the purple tubes. Not only does FORCE create folds but the forms or volumes of the body do as well. This is such an important aspect of clothing to help our drawings look like they possess mass.

Now we can see how the folds wrap around the anatomy of the body. The largest folds can be found around the bottom of the ribcage and the top of the right thigh. All of the openings on the clothes, such as the knees, seen at areas 3 and 4, the shoulders, and around the neck, give us clear orientations in the space of form. The bands around the upper arms and those around the wrist, labeled 1, finally give us the clues to volumes for this pose.

THIRD
LINES
TO
REPRESENT TENSION

In our last drawing for the section on form through general openings and wrapping, we can see the form of the mid-torso, which is actually depicted with the overlapping folds on the right side of the drawing of the torso. The hole of the neck is an echo of the form to reestablish that idea further up the torso of the model. In the bent leg, we see that the opening of the shorts imitates that ellipse. The lower leg has no fabric to support the orientation of the anatomy here so we do our best with that anatomy.

CLOTHING EXITS AND WRAPPING

The structure of clothes comes from the structure of our bodies coupled with the FORCE of gravity. If we have an idea of how clothes are built, then we know where to look at clothes to find evidence of how to draw forms using these areas of structure. Examples of the evidence are seams, zippers, pockets, and exit points such as cuffs, belt lines, and neck collars. Let's start at the top of the body with some hats.

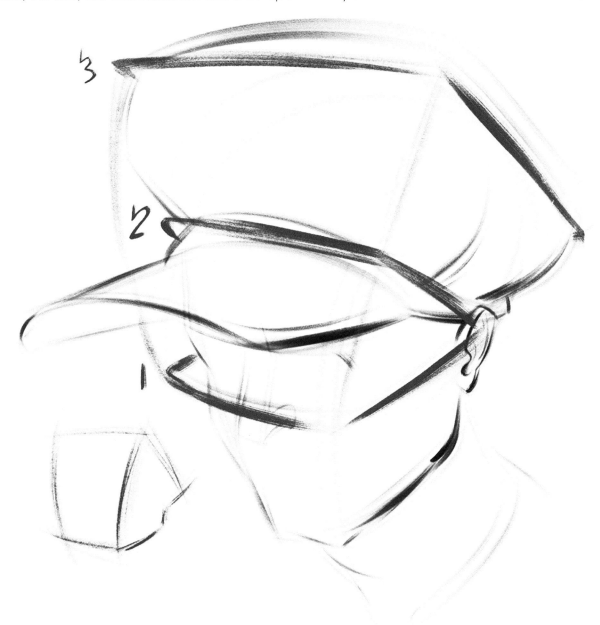

Using the color purple, see how I boxed out the drawing of the head at area 1. Then, the second purple line wraps the rim of the hat around the head and the third area gives us the top of the hat. Similar to an opened accordion, each angled plane helps the hat clarify the form of the head.

Above you can see the top form of the head at the purple ring and in the bottom right corner is a simple version of the head's perspective. Mritunjay drew clear structure in the head using the high peak of the eyebrow to define the edge between the front and side of the head.

In the prior hat drawings, I approached presenting clear perspective by drawing boxes. In this drawing, the tube of the hat is the primitive form most easily compared to this top hat. Do keep in mind that all primitives start with an understanding of drawing the box in perspective.

THE NECK LINE

As we move down the figure from the head, we reach the neck line, and here, we have the tube of the neck protruding out of the top plane of the shoulders and connecting to the base of the skull. The collar helps us get our head and neck through all styles of tops and therefore allow fabric to hang from our shoulders because of Gravity FORCE.

The collar above represents the roundness of the neck and its tubular integrity as shown with the purple tube and ring. Draw through the neck to make certain the ring you draw for the collar continues around the opaque back side of the neck.

Numerous styles of collars exist in the world of fashion, each with its own unique statement yet they all function the same way and can be used by the artist to clarify the tube of the neck. The two top collars also help us find the center of the chest or sternum.

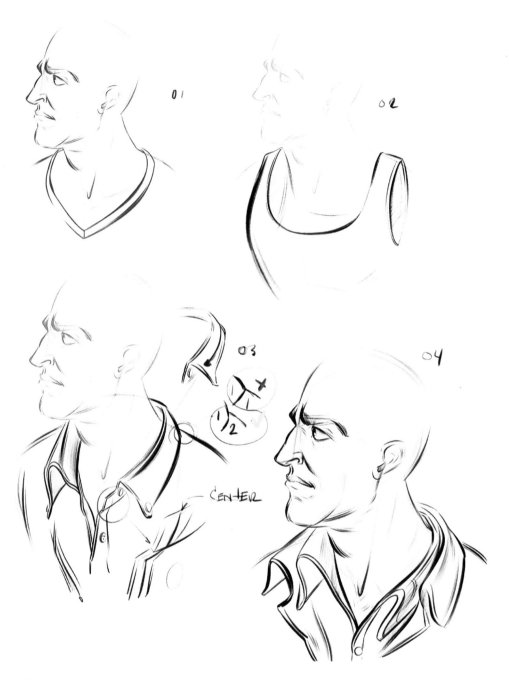

Here are a few illustrations showing male collars. Collar 01 created a clear center for the chest with the downward point of the V neck collar. Drawing 02 shows a wide tank top and that gives us a generic wide opening for the neck and head but does present us the holes for the area and their clear ellipses. Drawing 03 presents a very important point and that is to stay away from tangents when drawing the collars. The red X shows where the collar and the top edge of the shoulder align with one another. This removes depth and overlap. Below is another illustration presenting the remedy for this problem and therefore a stacking of forms in space. We also see here the center line down the front of the collar for the placement of the buttons.

The scarf in this drawing is more complex than the simple collar and still presents the clear tube of the neck. Stay aware of the use of the apparel no matter how complicated its folds may be. The ends of the scarf show us the evidence of gravity pulling downward on the fabric.

THE ARM

At the base of the arm where it meets the torso, you can find clothes that will show this connection in space. Typically, this is found in sleeveless tops like tank tops. The ellipse of the sleeveless opening of the tank top makes for clear form. Ellipses of form can also be found in short sleeve shirts, three quarter sleeve shirts, and then long sleeve, sharing with us the form of the wrist.

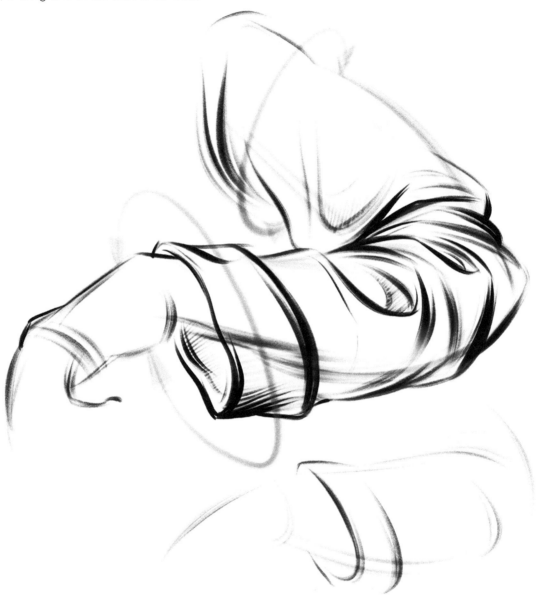

Witness the power of the ellipses created at the wrists constructing the exit from the shirt and allowing us to depict clear form!

At the wrist, the hole, or exit, offers a great opportunity to clearly show the form of the arm into the hand. Also, observe the folds above the wrists define the correct ellipses.

15

It is easy to over draw and confuse the direction of the folds in the lower arm, since folds pile up here in loose clothing so make sure to set them up to support the exit of the wrists and hand through an understanding of perspective. Try to redraw this illustration to gain a better understanding of how FORCE and rhythm move through space clearly defined by the folds.

THE WAIST LINE

The largest ellipse in the figure is found at the waist. I recommend starting with a more box like structure to define the pelvis and then learn how the top of that box can be transformed into an ellipse. This area of the body is essential for presenting the form of the figure. The pelvis and ribcage are the two main forms of the figure and here is where we define one of them.

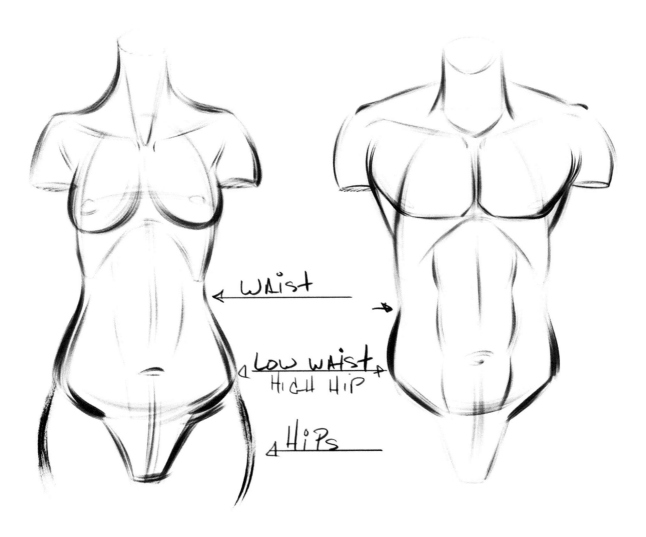

For me, the pelvis causes a great deal of confusion in fashion. I thought it was important to add this comparative illustration for two reasons; the first is that artists have challenges drawing the difference between male and female anatomy. The second reason to publish the drawing is to discuss the gender differences and terms used in fashion, starting with the waist. In fashion, the waist is located where I labeled it within the drawings. In speaking for myself and probably most men, I consider my waist at the top of my pelvis, which is also what I would call the top of my hips. In fashion, especially for woman, their hips are at the bottom of the pelvis, at the peak of the greater trochanter where women's widest measurement can be found. Ugh, so confusing. In men's fashion, there were pants designed to sit at our fashion waist, but today, we wear our pants at the top of the pelvis or low waist. Women on the other hand can purchase pants that rest at the waist, low waist, and even at the hip. So many different terms describe these locations such as low rider, hip hugger, high waisted, and low waisted.

Notice the clear direction of the torso here due to the ellipses of the rib cage and pelvis. The top of the shorts clearly exemplifies their orientation in space. In fact, see how all the ellipses point in the same direction within three-dimensional space.

By Michael Mattesi

Look at the bottom of the shirt and see that the edge creates an S curve. The left side of the pelvis, and on the back, the curve goes upward showing the direction of the back's form.

By the time, we move down to the top of the skirt, we have a simple, single, downward curve that shows us the direction in space of the pelvis.

The waist is the largest of exits from a piece of apparel. It is where tops meet bottoms, and where shirts and blouses meet jeans, pants, and skirts.

Above is a waistline showing us the volume found there. Remember what we learned earlier about gravity, and how the waist line is where clothes hang from the hips.

By drawing through the figure, we get a better understanding of the full ellipse and column in this region of the body. It seems here that we can see down into the space of the pelvis.

In this more dynamic drawing, we can again see the clarity of volume at the waistline. This moment helps us see that the ellipse tilts downward, and then, the upper body bends upward and away from our eyes over the surface of the model's back. The change in three-dimensional space adds much drama to the figure drawing and pose.

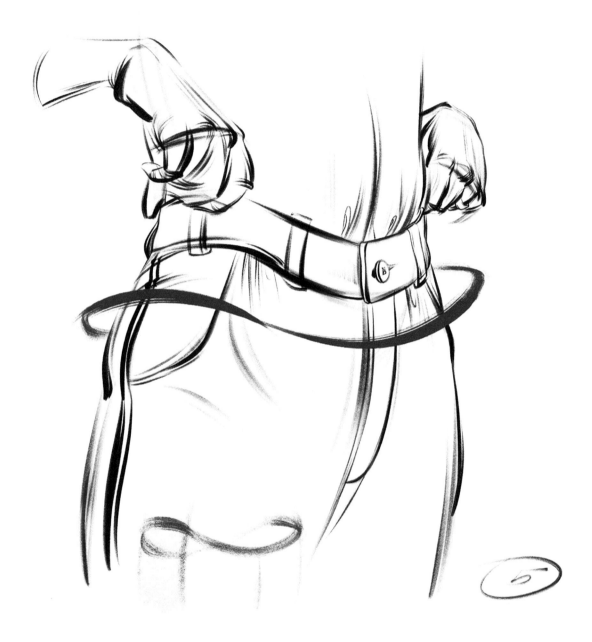

The waist line here is sophisticated in that the simple ellipse now lifts upward on the sides and downward in the front and back of it. This version of form is still built off of the ellipse which in turn is built off of a rectangular plane. The purple diagram in the bottom left corner shows the importance of understanding the turning edges of the waist.

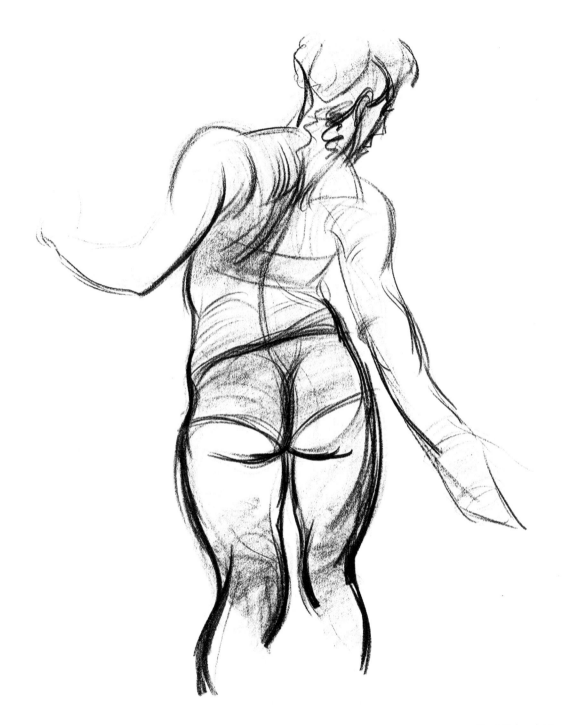

By Michael Mattesi

The top of the shorts at the waistline curves away from us and you can see a change in curve direction at the bottom of the model's top. The two opposite curves show us the opposing orientations of the two forms as the model stands in what I call a C torso pose.

THE PANTS HEM

As we move down again, away from the waist, we arrive at mid-thigh where most shorts end. Shorts are an excellent apparel for showing the orientation in space of the upper legs. In this illustration, we see that each leg is pointing in the opposite direction of the other.

Now, we have reached the bottom of the leg where we find the hem of full-length pants. This pair of pants has an elastic band in the hem causing a tighter ellipse above the ankle. Look at the size difference between the two feet. This immediately defines depth in the drawing along with the volumes created by the ellipse due to the hems.

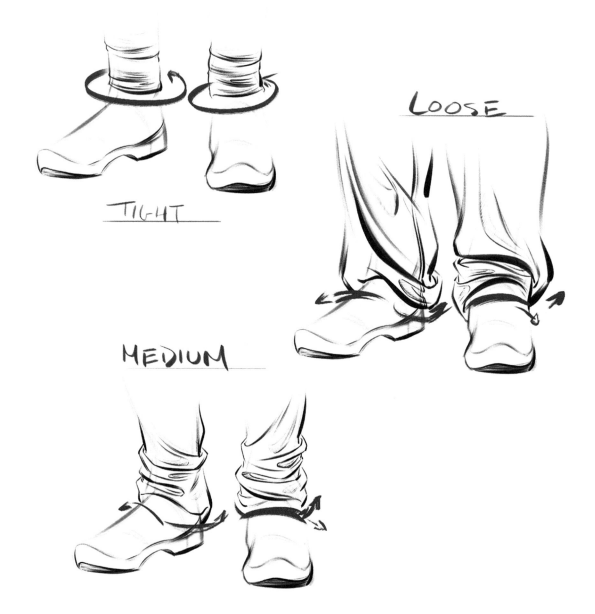

LOOSE

TIGHT

MEDIUM

Across different fits of clothing, we can understand that there are some changes in how the forms are explained. In tight-fitting pants, they wrap around the ankle. Medium and loose-fit pants curve over the top of the foot and down around the sides of the ankles.

Moving from the hems of pants, we arrive at last of ellipses that present form in the figure, the lower leg is where we find the top of socks, and tops of shoes, boots sandals, etc. Above, the elastic top of the sock hugs the lower leg creating a clear ellipse for the X folds below to wrap around.

The vertically most low piece of apparel, are shoes. The S double loop can be discovered here over the top of the foot front and below the angle found on the side of the foot, similar to the fit of medium and loose pants. The purple diagram shows the ellipses that the double S loop portrays.

By Michael Mattesi

In this final drawing for our section on how the form and structure of cloths helps us draw a more solid figure, we have Chris wear a loose-fitting shirt and pants further presenting some bold folds in the figure. From the form of the folds themselves as seen in area 3 to the tube found in area 4, folds and exits help develop orientations in space! Area 3 also uses surface line to further define the solidity of the planes of the clothing.

SEAMS AND STRUCTURAL ACCOUTREMENTS

In the last chapter, we discussed the ellipses of clothing that are created due to the structures of our anatomy. In an effort to create these holes, the pieces of fabric known as Flats, get sewn together, and are commonly known as seams. In addition to seams, buttons and button holes, snaps, buckles, rings, beads, zippers, and labels all make up the anatomy of clothing.

Our apparel is created primarily by cutting fabric in patterns called flats. These flats are sewn together to create our clothing. Sometimes, the patterns call for left- and right-side flats such as pants. Sometimes, in pants for example, the patterns call for left- and right-side flats. Notice that your pants have a seam running down the center in the front and back and down the inseam and outside of the legs. Therefore, there are four parts to the pants.

Many seams create clear form in this image. Look at all the shirt sleeves, the father and son's clothing present us. Notice the seam down the center of the back on the child's overalls. The boy's sleeveless top shows the ellipse from which his arm emerges and, in the father's, long sleeve shirt we can use the seam at the shoulder to execute the same job.

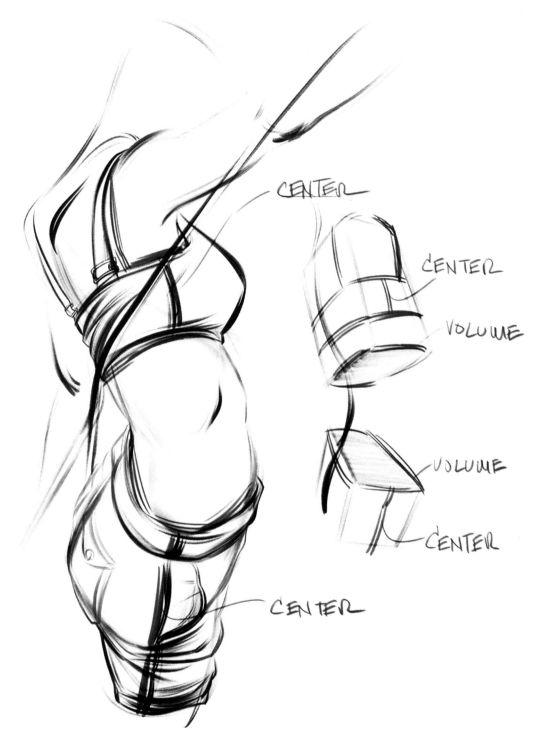

CENTER

CENTER

VOLUME

VOLUME

CENTER

CENTER

Shown with all the purple lines, there is alot of form to discover here. On the right, we have a diagram of the ribcage and pelvis boxes. I want you to see how the model's top and bottom apparel help present those two forms. The seams down the center of these garments help to even further clarify those boxes.

Again, the seams at the top of the sleeves help present the exit of the arms from the torso. The seam down the side of the torso is a great center line for defining the side plane. The seam across the top of the back defines a shape called the 'yoke.' The yoke typically fits over the upper back. Not to be confused with the wooden harness of a plow or a control column found in planes, this yoke creates further structure to a garment and originated in western style clothing.

Once again, we have the seam for the short sleeve of the shirt, the seam down the center of the side of the torso and a new seam, and the center at the top plane of the shoulder girdle. Use these seams as an opportunity to create form, understand the parts of ths garment and their shapes, and how when brought together they create this short sleeve shirt.

Seams can be found in garments for the legs as well. Here we see them down the center of the sides of the legs which, in turn, help us understand their structure. Take notice of the slight turn of the front leg from the knee to the ankle.

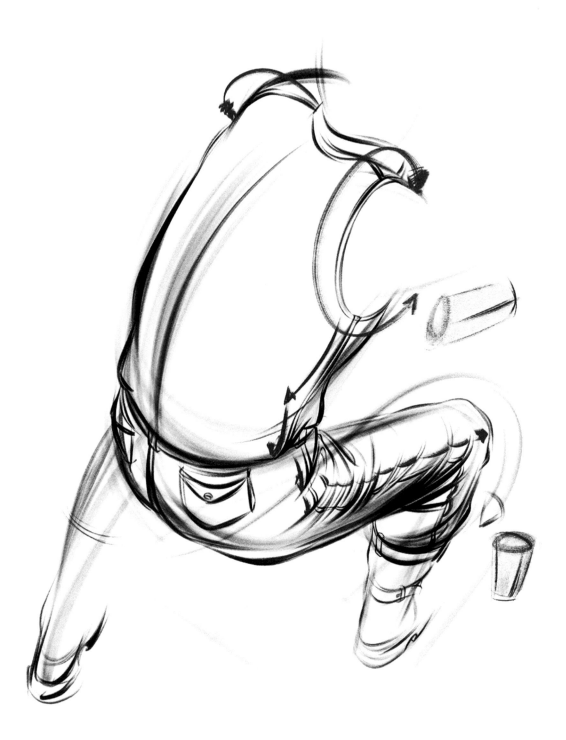

This sleeveless shirt shows us the hole the arm exits through, and the seam runs down the side of the torso and we can also see that center line continue down the middle of the side of the leg, throughout the length of the pants, all accomplished through a deep amount of space.

Let's view these hands as a microcosm of the figure. Many FORCES and forms can be found here. Seams down the centers of either side of the hand convey structure and how they were built with a front and back half. The holes for the fingers are excellent at showing the different orientations in space the fingers point.

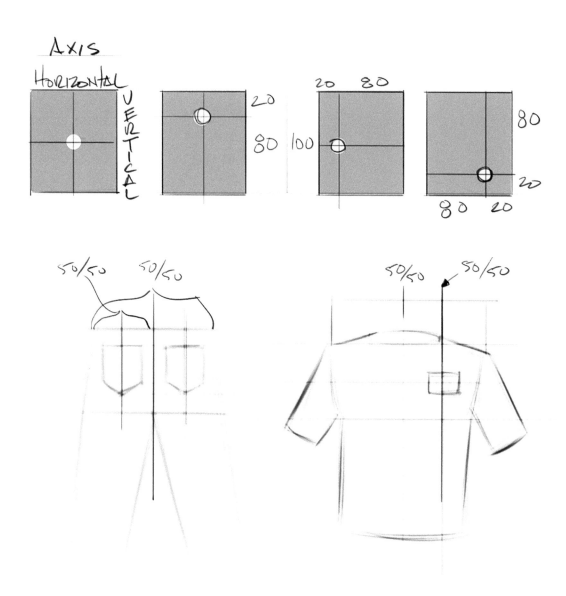

How are buttons zippers, pockets, and more located on apparel? I look at the flats as graphic shapes, which helps when deciding where on a garment to place buttons, zippers, pockets, etc. It also allows me to design, by choice, the layout of these areas on the clothing.

In the top left corner, we start with a shape that is almost a perfect square. This shape has width and height measurements. Knowledge of these two measurements means we can break them down in symmetrical or asymmetrical ratios. In the second image, I divided the height by 80/20 ratio of 100%. The third image shows the vertical height split in half, 50/50. The horizontal width, however, is split by 80/20. That makes for an interesting placement of the button. The fourth image splits the shape by 80/20 along both axis.

We can continue this idea and apply it to the pockets on the back of a pair of pants. Most of the time this is done with 50/50 or symmetry splits. The same goes for the location of this chest badge on the left pectoralis.

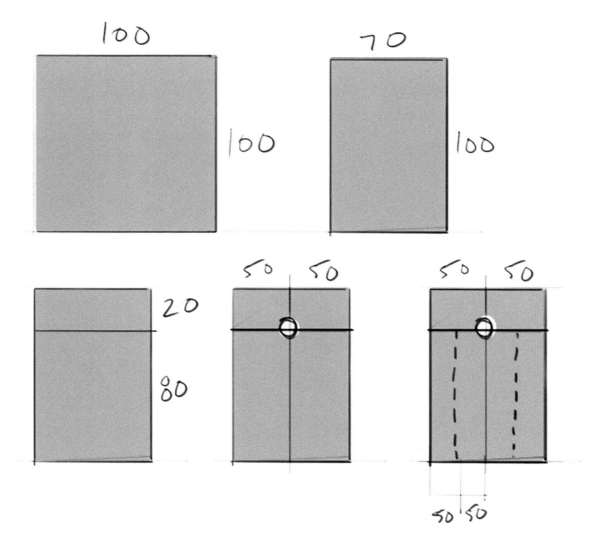

Let's take this concept to a single pocket and see how it can be used. First, we take a box and break it down to a 70%–30% split, horizontally. Then, I contrast the overall proportions further to an 80/20 split. This creates a narrow flap across the top of the pocket. Then, we split the pocket 50/50 from the left to right side. Lastly, we take each of those shapes and break them into 50/50 splits again for the placement of some decorative stiches.

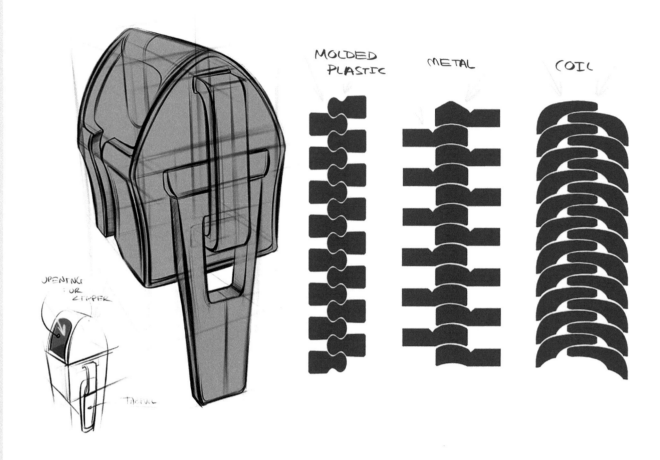

MOLDED PLASTIC

METAL

COIL

OPENING FOR ZIPPER

FABRIC

I love the simple and effective function of the zipper and how it brings fabric together. As the slider is fed the teeth of the zipper, they are merged on top of one another snapping them into place. Just for some fun edification, we have three different types of zippers: molded plastic, metal, and coil zippers. They present a cool detail you can added strategically to your clothing drawings.

Buttons and zippers can be Applied and/or Gravity anchor points. Here, I am pulling the shirt upward with my hand which is therefore an Applied FORCE Anchor Point. The bottom left side near my hip is a Gravity Anchor Point. In the middle of this tug of war is the poor shirt button. In reference to the Applied FORCE Anchor Point the button is a Gravity Anchor Point and for the Gravity Anchor Point of the hip, it is an Applied FORCE Anchor Point since it is pulling upward with the hand.

ASSIGNMENTS

1. Learn to draw four-point perspective.

2. Then become an expert at drawing a box at any angle. Try to slowly rotate it to find those challenging moments and solve the strong angles.

3. Use that box knowledge to now define primitives/basic forms: Pyramid, cone, tube, and sphere.

4. Take this information to the figure by creating turning edges across the torso and all limbs. Add cross contours to help clarify the direction in space of all forms with ellipses.

5. Elevate the attention to detail by now sculpting the forms.

6. Bring these concepts to drawing fabric and clothing. Start by drawing the exits or openings on clothes such as hats, the collar, cuffs, the pants' hem, top of socks, shoe entry, etc.

7. Now bring in the concept of seams and see how the clothes are made to support construction.

SHAPE

We started with Directional and Applied FORCES. Now, those lines come to create something greater than themselves, shapes, illustrated with gray tone. This is a big mental shift that occurs, and the concept of drawings shapes instead of thinking about the lines creating rhythms in the figures and the clothes that they wear.

Above are three NON-FORCEFUL shapes. All three shapes are symmetrical, and this prohibits FORCE to exit these shapes in a diagonal manner into another shape that can redirect FORCE and create rhythm. On the left is 'the sausage.' FORCE pinches at the top and bottom of the shape, trapped, with no exit. The second shape is 'the pipe' and as you can see FORCE can now escape but only in a straight line so it does not allow FORCE to push out in an angle. Loss of the angle stops rhythm from being created. The last shape is 'the pimple.'

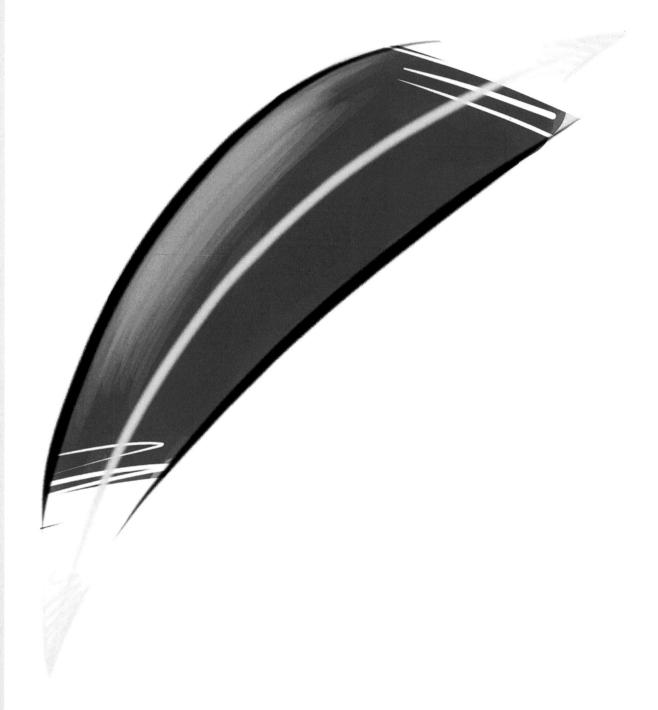

Here is our FORCE-Shape developed with a curve of FORCE on one side and a straighter line on the other. Remember, we are now using line to create shape, the gray area between the lines. You can see here that the shape dynamically directs FORCE on more of an angle out of the shape which can then later be picked up by another FORCE-Shape and two combined will create rhythms.

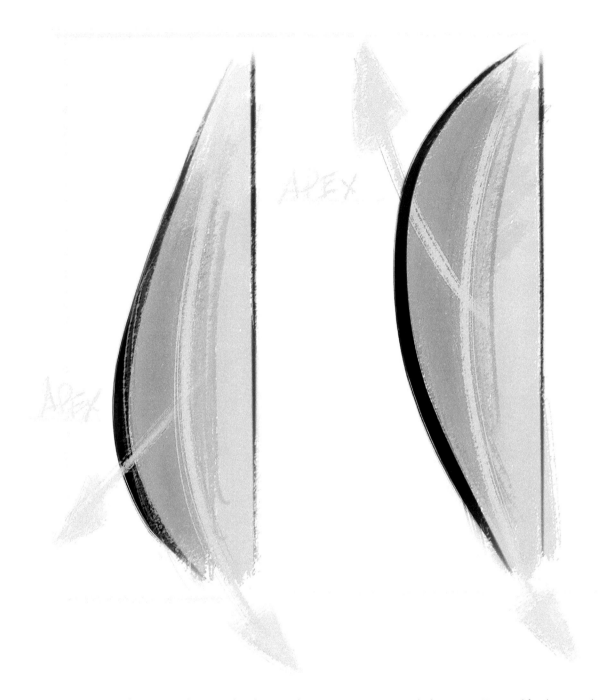

To bring more specificity to such a simple abstract shape, we can start with the apex. To simplify choices, think about the apex as either low medium or high along the length of the FORCE curve line. Look at the gray shape of FORCE and see how is has been affected by this change in apex. The low apex makes the shape feel like there is weight hanging on the bottom of the shape and the high apex seems almost powerful or confident as the high curve defies the FORCE of gravity.

Now push form back into these FORCEFUL shapes, which seems to transform into blobs, FORCE-Blobs. The combination of FORCE, Form, and Shape is a powerful trifecta. The FORCE-Shape combines FORCE and shape into FORCEFUL shapes and with an injection of form, we can truly draw anything organic and rhythmic and keep the drawn volumes.

When we apply the ideas of Directional and Applied FORCES to the figure, we achieve drama, rhythm, and beauty along with function in the entire body and pose. Comprehension of this system of rhythm and FORCES allows us to better depict them when drawing fabric as clothing. Above you can see that the two strongest areas of Applied FORCE are the shoulder and hip. The blue arrows show the Directional FORCES that connect these moments.

The moment any type of clothing or apparel is added to the model, there is an opportunity to see form more clearly. The blues shapes define the silhouettes of the upper and lower legs. Since anatomy and FORCES are consistent, over time you can learn what the shapes look like from different angles which helps better understand the way clothes rest on the body and shapes clothes create. The purple line above shows a partial ellipse with an upward curve that suggests the roundness and volume of the model's core. On her ribcage, you also will notice she is wearing a top that shows the volume of her upper torso.

Notice the column-like strength of the model's right leg, and the fluid 'S' rhythm of the torso flowing over that stability. The clothing fabric will stretch and fold based on gravity and the FORCES generated by the model's pose.

See if you can identify the FORCE Shapes utilized to create this fluid drawing of the female model. The first shape to find is that of the ribcage, then the core and pelvis. After those shapes, find the upper and lower leg shapes. Each of the feet also exhibits clear FORCE-Shape design. The way to find these shapes is to first understand the Directional FORCES that create the figures rhythms.

By Michael Mattesi

Shape is a powerful tool when drawing clothing as well. The blue shape of the leg is comprised of two FORCE Shapes in Chris's pants. Each contains one of the curves to the right of the leg. Shape allows you to cut through the noise and find FORCE to create more clear, appealing design.

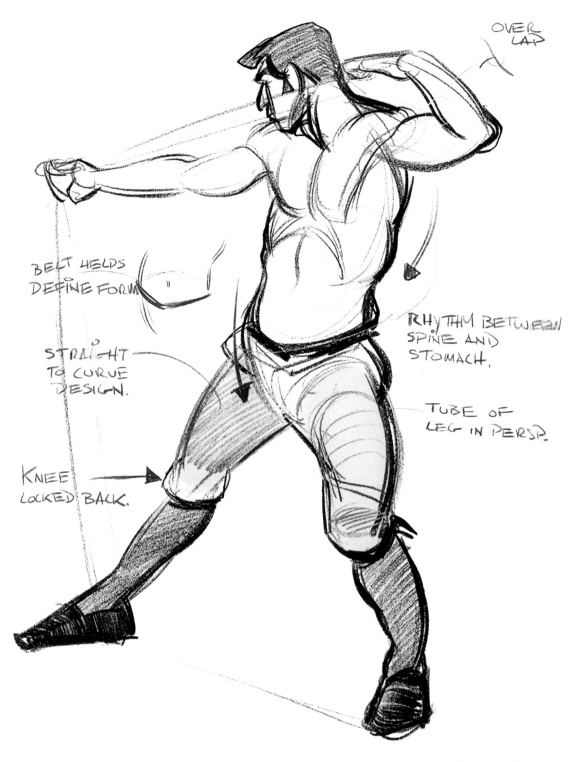

OVER
LAP

BELT HELPS
DEFINE FORM

STRAIGHT
TO CURVE
DESIGN.

KNEE
LOCKED BACK.

RHYTHM BETWEEN
SPINE AND
STOMACH.

TUBE OF
LEG IN PERSP.

By Michael Mattesi

These pants are a tight fit to the legs, so the FORCE Shapes found in the anatomy are presented in the clothing as well. Here, you can see the immediate benefit of knowing what the FORCE Shapes are for the anatomy of the body.

This concept of FORCE Shapes can be scaled down to individual or groups of folds in the fabric. Above are two major shapes clearly showing two groups of J-folds through their shapes. Notice the Gravity Anchor Point and how the fabric hangs from that moment twisting over to the Applied FORCE Anchor Point creating two appealing shapes.

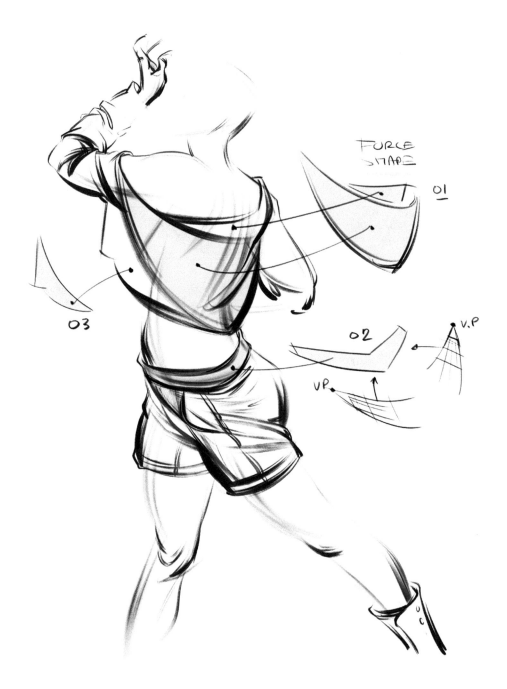

Area 01 shows the two main shapes that move across the model's back, hanging from the Applied FORCE Anchor Point of the left shoulder and defining a J-Fold that hooks around the right side of the body. In area 02, see how shape also creates depth through the mere pinching of a shape. The narrower far corners fool our eyes into thinking that the belt moves into space due to the diminishing size of the belt's shapes. The shape is largest at the location where it is closest to us. Area 03 shows the last small FORCE-Shape that hangs from the left shoulder.

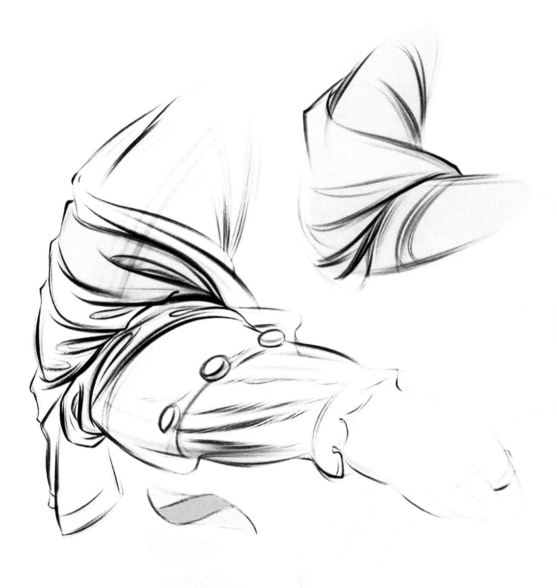

In the top right illustration, there are three main shapes, the upper arm, the lower arm, and the group of folds moving from the back of the upper arm to the bottom of the wrist of the lower arm. In the second drawing, I highlighted one of the three main folds at the elbow area. Below this drawing are three simple blue-shaped diagrams. The top one shows the full S-rhythm of that fold. Below it are the two separate shapes that created the S-shape found in that particular fold.

Lots of FORCE Shapes are being created from all of the folds found in this long sleeve shirt on a very simple model pose. Each of these shapes has one stronger FORCE-edge and a somewhat straighter side. Visualizing these shapes helps you quickly draw appealing shaped folds with great efficiency.

ASSIGNMENTS

1. Memorize the NON-FORCEFUL Shapes, and go on the hunt for the FORCEFUL Shape.
2. Practice drawing FORCE-Blobs to better understand how FORCE-Shape and form are combined to give you all the drawing information you need.
3. Draw FORCE Shapes with high, middle, and low Applied FORCE-apexes for variety.
4. Draw multiple FORCE-Blobs connected to one another to create FORCE-Blob rhythms.
5. Bring FORCE-Shape to drawing the nude figure.
6. Notice the FORCE-Shape in the silhouette of clothing and in the shape of folds!

FOLD TYPES

Our bodies are capable of many different actions and poses. The fabrics and garments we wear serve many different purposes. The folds generated by them are the clues to Gravity and Applied FORCES, within the pose. Since there are many variables, we must understand many different types of folds.

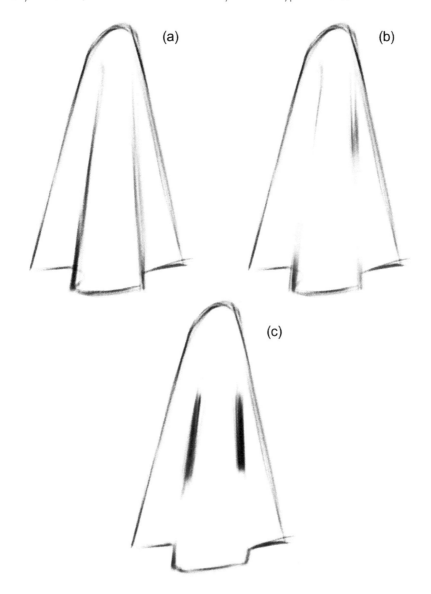

(a)

(b)

(c)

When drawing folds, the most informative way to draw them is from the starting point, through the length of the fold, to its other end. We can see this in the first illustration. The second illustration can work as well. Often, the fold will disappear across a surface through the mid region. What does not work well is the third example. This proves out that we need the start and end which are actually the anchor points or edge of the fabric.

DOI: 10.1201/9781351049467-4

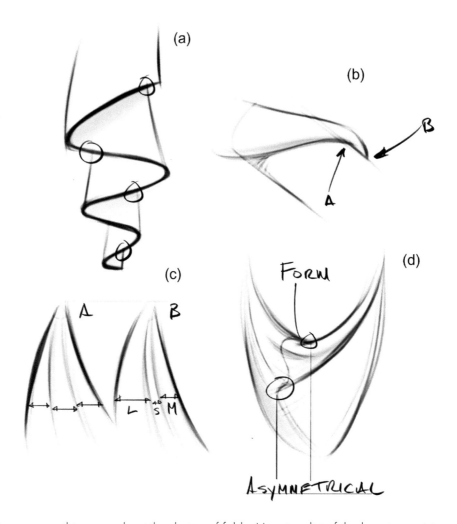

(a)

(b)

B

A

(c)

FORM

(d)

A   B

L   S M

ASYMNETRICAL

There is a lot to cover on this page about the design of folds. Here is a list of the learning points per drawing:

1. Very often you will simply draw the edge of a fabric, it might be a dress, a skirt, a shawl, or a scarf. Make certain to create clear, overlapping moments as seen within the circles. Also notice that each major surface of the folds does not align with the contour of the surface below. Watch out for tangents, and define clear overlaps.

2. To create clarity, when fabric wraps around a form giving the fabric thickness, offset the edge of the fabric that rests on the edge of the body's contour. Location A is further up the contour than location B, and the space between the two allows us to think there is a thickness to this fabric as it wraps around the tubular form.

3. Keep the width of folds varied. The triangular shape on the left exhibits folds of equal distances. On the right triangle, we can see that I changed the width of the three folds making one small, then medium, and then large in their varied widths.

4. Always be aware of the form of the fabric's folds as shown with the center form line. When you draw folds, pay attention to creating asymmetrical peaks or apexes to once again escape inorganic, symmetrical design.

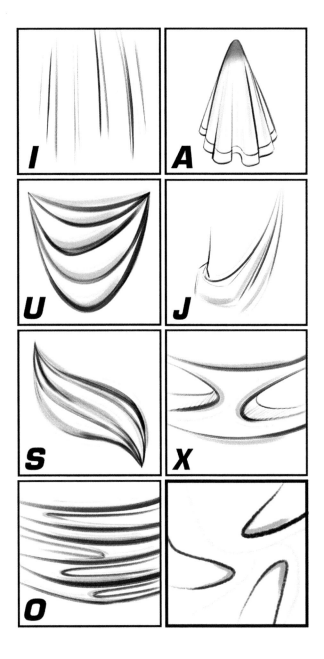

Above is our FORCE Folds Chart showing eight primary folds. I have distilled the folds to letters of the alphabet that are visually similar. This will make them easier to remember. It might seem that there are endless types of folds; however, when we understand their function, we realize that there are similarities among them, simplifying the number of varieties. Each symbol of a fold type shows the black lines you would use to illustrate them. Tension FORCE lines present the abstract flow moving through the folds. The orange areas show the Applied FORCES that push into either weight or internal body FORCE.

In this chapter, I will deeply discuss each fold type and draw common examples of where they are found in apparel and poses. These fold type stickers are placed throughout the rest of the book to teach you how to see and label folds that you will find in future model reference. My goal is that you will recognize common and repetitive systems of folds.

The I-Fold

There is a beautiful progression that occurs across the I-, A-, U-, J-, and S-Folds. The I-Fold is typically known as the pipe fold. Simple, straight, vertical lines hang from single or numerous anchor points above, while gravity pulls the fabric down to the ground. This fold can also occur across the body if the anchor points are separated.

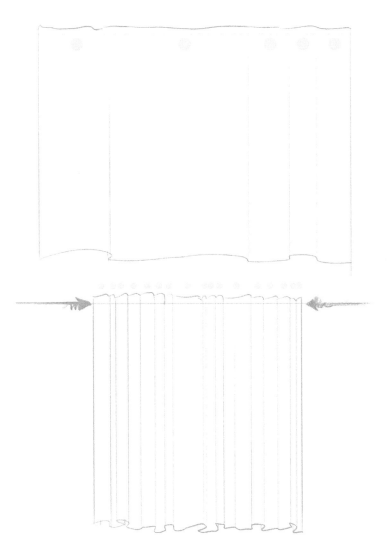

I-Folds increase in numbers as Applied FORCES gather fabric and allow it to fold more often. Each fold creates a new Gravity Anchor Point. A curtain is a great example of the I-Fold. The orange arrows show us the Applied FORCES. Now let's bring that to some clothing.

The orange arrows show us the Applied FORCES and a curtain is a great example of the I-Fold. Now let's bring that to some clothing.

Skirts and most dresses are the most common articles of clothing that display the I-Fold. Above you can see a very casual flair on this skirt presenting a few Gravity Anchor Points at the waist. You will also notice how Tension FORCES pull the fabric down toward its lowest edge.

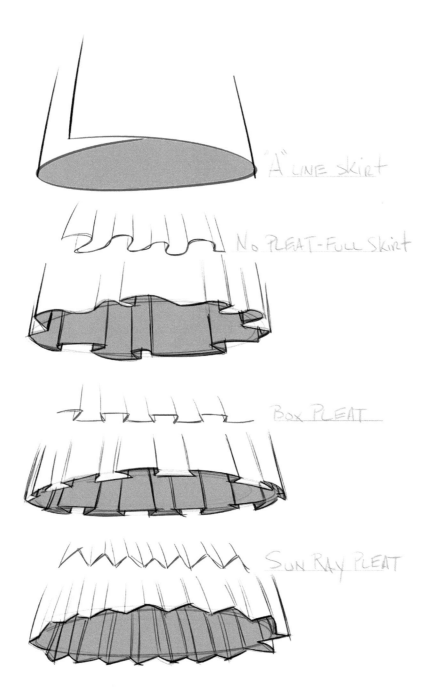

"A" LINE SKIRT

No PLEAT-FULL SKIRT

Box PLEAT

SUN RAY PLEAT

Look at different pleat structures that can be found in a skirt. Each of these develops Gravity Anchor Points at the waistline and direct the fabric down to the hem in varying ways, from very fluid styles like those of a loose skirt, to more rigid styles, such as the box pleat. Start a drawing like these with an ellipse to define the perspective and form that build the skirt.

By Michael Mattesi

In my 2-5 minute drawings, I used the pleated skirt to help define volume around the waist and pelvis. I used the lines of the pleats to vertically wrap around the surfaces found on the body.

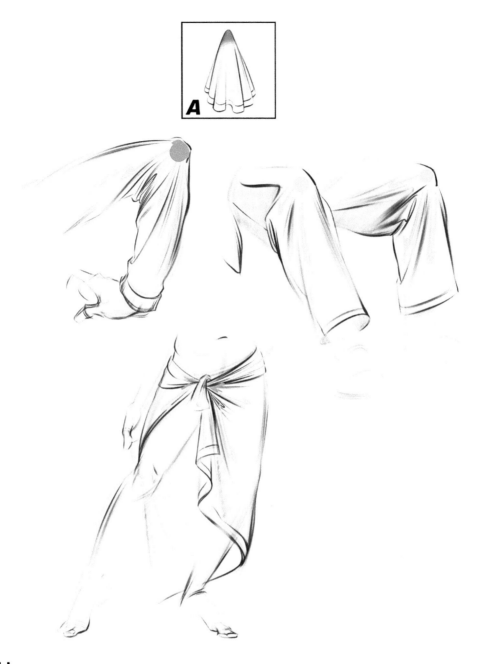

The A-Fold

Moving on from numerous and single anchor points found in the I-Fold category, we now have the A-Fold with one anchor point! When it comes to the power of the Gravity Anchor Point, as seen at the knees, fabric hangs from a single point. Based on the thickness of the fabric, the **angled** flare of the fold's bottom is narrow or wide. Applied FORCE Anchor Points can also cause this type of folding when a joint, such as a knee or elbow, bends. The stretched side of the bend will present the Applied FORCE Anchor Point that creates the A-Fold.

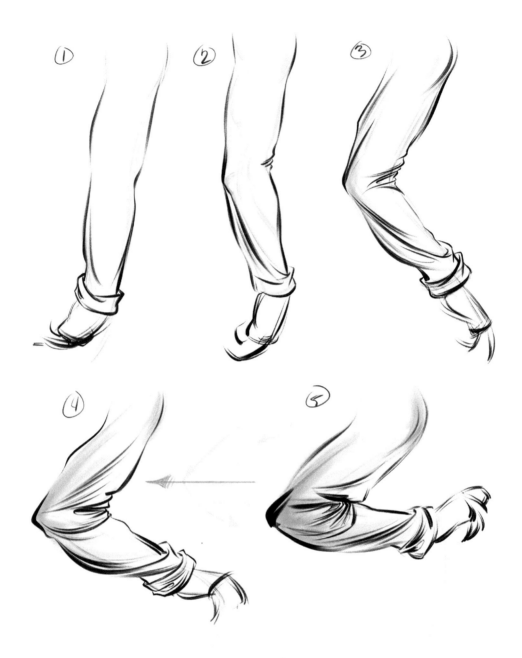

Let's dig deeper into one of the most common presentations of the A-Fold, the bending of the elbow. As Applied FORCE, shown in orange, increases in the elbow, the ramifications of that FORCE cause Tension FORCES to increase further and further out to the shoulder and the wrist. The blue Tension FORCES clearly connect the Applied FORCES.

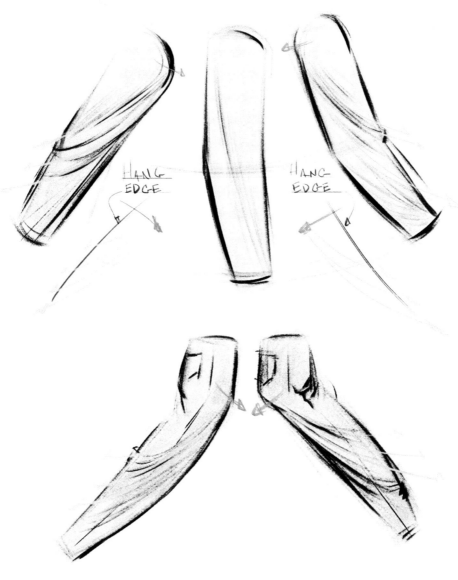

In an effort to continue simplification, the sleeve and the pant leg are very similar in shape and form so let's compare them. The top left image shows the arm turned toward the back and below is the leg turned to the back. So, the Applied FORCE Anchor Point can be found in both at their front right edge near the shoulder and pelvis. This A-Fold set up then causes Tension Folds to pull from the anchor point pull in the opposite direction. The same ideas occur when we flip the direction of the arm and leg and move it toward the front. The Applied FORCE Anchor Point can be found in the back of the shoulder or the rear end. Then, the Tension FORCES pull from that point to the front of the arm or leg. Between the drawings of the arms, you can find further simplified diagrams. The black line in each is the edge that the clothing hangs from. Then, the anchor points and FORCES to their jobs on the fabric of the respective garments.

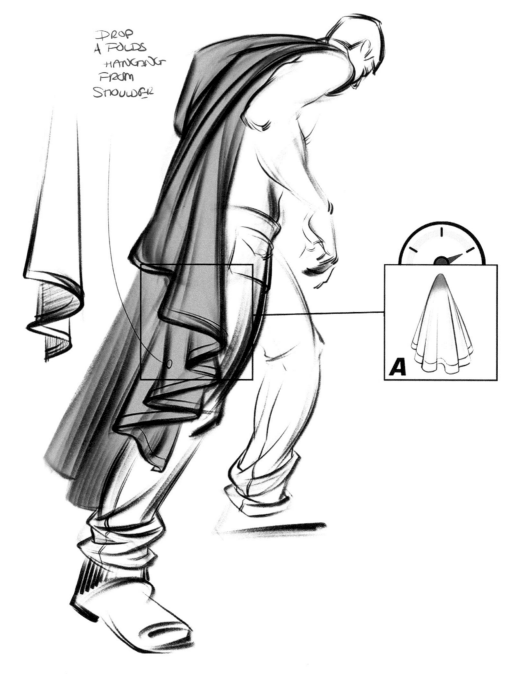

DROP
A FOLDS
HANGING
FROM
SHOULDER

A

Recall our page on design ideas. Here is a cloak with that ribbon-like edge. Notice the clear overlaps that help define the space that the bottom of the cloak occupies. All the A-Folds hang off the model's back in layers creating that great, fluid edge of the cape. This fabric must be relatively thin and fast since the curves on the fluid edge are pretty narrow or acute.

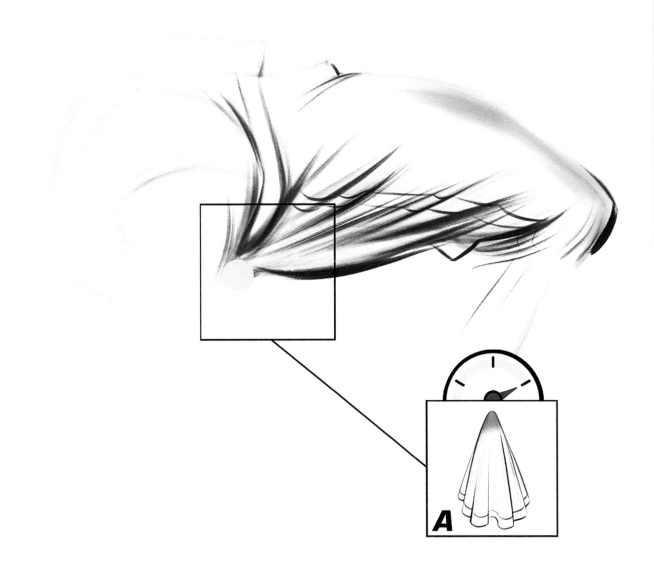

A common A-Fold situation can be found in pants where they pull from the bottom of the pelvis and up to the front and top of the thigh. This diagonal pull is a strong indicator of how great Applied FORCE in the thigh creates the Applied FORCE Anchor Point there. Feel all that tension across the leg.

By Michael Mattesi

See if you can now find the A-Fold. My daughter Makenna's hand grabs the long, puffy vest, and in doing so creates an Applied FORCE A-Fold. The bigger and looser the garment, the more pronounced the folds will be.

The U-Fold

Moving from the A-Fold that is defined with a single anchor point, we move to the U-Fold, also known as the diaper fold due to its iconic visual. Gravity pulls fabric from two Gravity Anchor Points causing this drop or hang in between the points. Depending on the speed of the fabric, this fold can also create what looks like a V Fold.

The back of this pose shows us two U-Folds which support the spatial orientation of the pelvis bottom and both of the legs. Folds around the torso do an excellent job of wrapping and defining dramatic space for us in this pose. The U-Fold is a great opportunity for you to work on your asymmetrical apex practice which we discussed earlier.

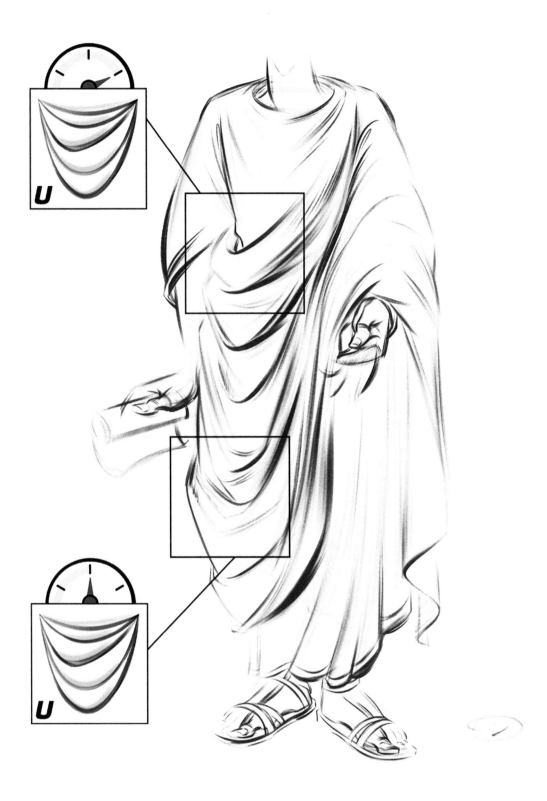

Loose fit clothing is primarily about draping. Draping brings out copious amounts of U-Folds since fabric typically hangs from two Gravity Anchor Points as we can see in the illustration above. How can this drawing be improved? The shapes of the folds could be designed to be more varied as we discussed earlier.

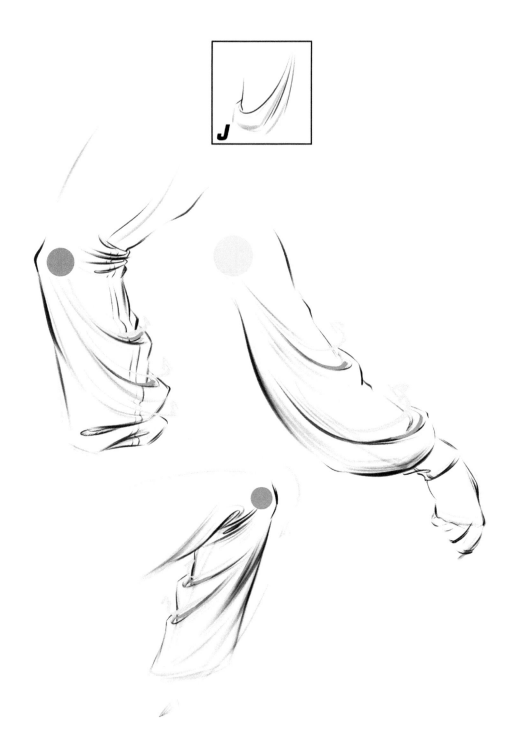

The J-Fold

The J-Fold is an A-Fold with an anchor point that coaxes the fabric to hang in a hook where fabric wraps around the anatomy of the body. At that point, the fabric comes to rest. Above are some examples of fabric hanging from Gravity and Applied FORCE Anchor Points of an A-Fold that wraps around an arm or leg. So, a J-Fold can come from a Gravity or Applied FORCE Anchor Point, and wraps around a form.

In front of the chest, what at first appears to be a large A-Fold becomes two J-Folds upon closer examination. On the leg, we find O-Folds since they have numerous Applied FORCE Anchor Points that pull around the thigh. Without the pull, we may not have encountered them, but with that tension, we have folds that pull around the leg.

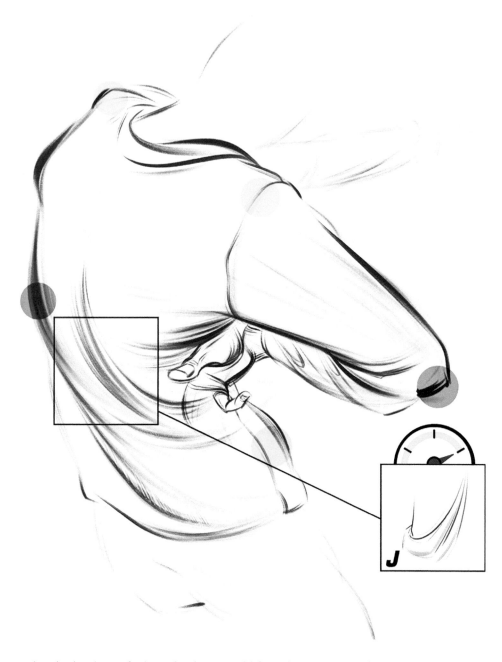

Moving around to the back, we find another large J-Fold from the Gravity Anchor Point that is found at the base of the neck, and then moves around to the top of the right hip. Also, notice the A-Fold that pulls between the Applied FORCE Anchor Point and the Gravity Anchor Point in the right shoulder.

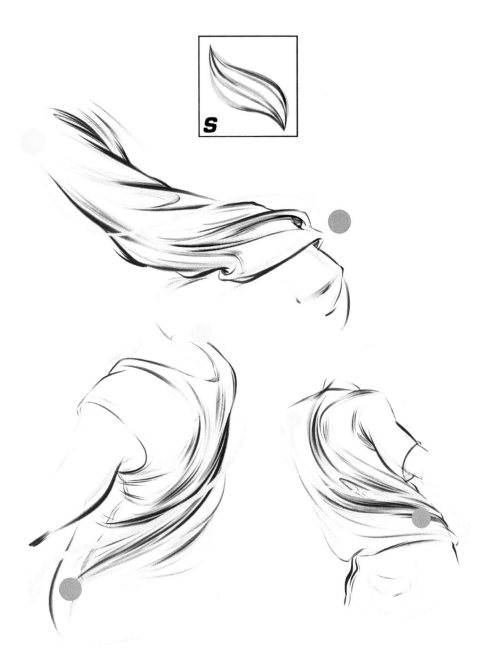

The S-Fold

The S-Fold moves one step beyond the J-Fold. Instead of the fabric only hooking around a form and resting, as the J-Fold does, the S-Fold continues the flow of rhythm around the anatomy. This rhythm, as seen in the examples above, is commonly created through rotation or torque within the figure, or a movement caused by the figure. It typically starts with a Gravity Anchor Point and then pulls as it is rotated around a form by an Applied FORCE Anchor Point.

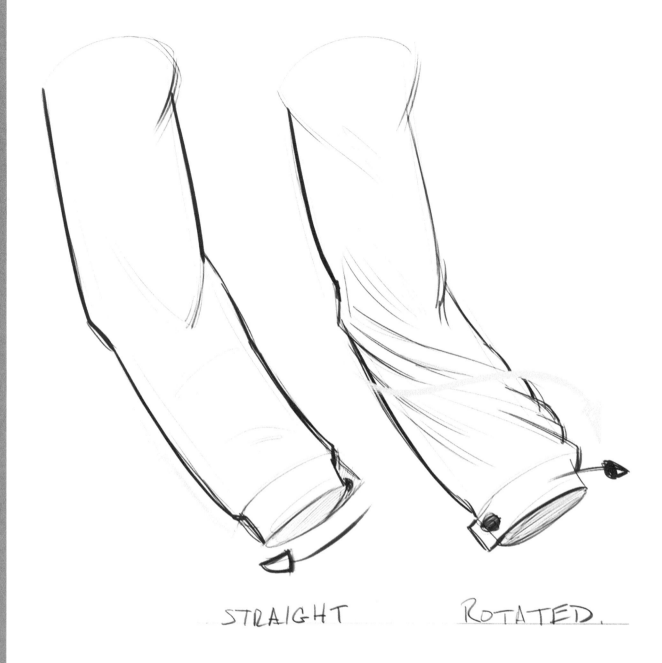

STRAIGHT   ROTATED.

Here are 'before and after' illustrations, visually portraying the idea of how the S-Fold can come from anatomical FORCE rotation. These drawings are of a right arm rotating inward. This action pulls the fabric over and around the forearm so Directional FORCE lines align with the tension found between the elbow and rotated wrist.

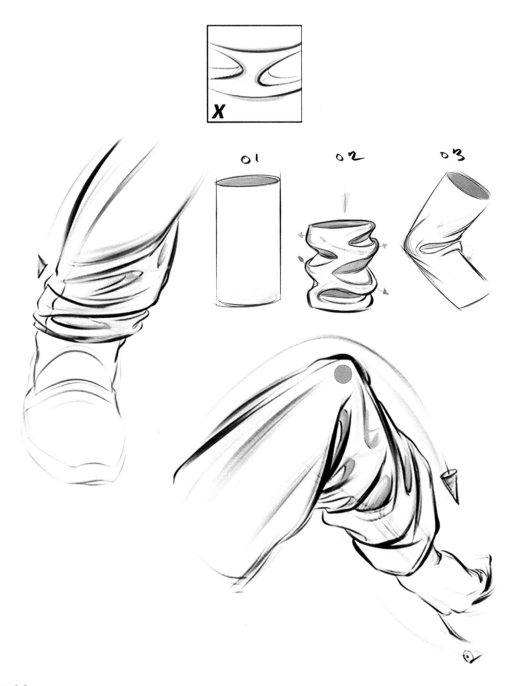

The X-Fold

Nearing the end of folds, we encounter the X-Fold. The space between the folds increases either due to the thickness of the fabric itself or the fabric has not been compressed into an O-Fold yet. As you can see, this fold type is normally found at the base of pants at the ankle or at the wrist due to pushed up sleeves. Drawing 01 shows a piece of fabric in the form of a tube. When the fabric drapes on a tube, it creates these X-Folds. I call them X-Folds due to the X like ridge pattern they create between the inverted folds. Drawing 03 shows us how a bent elbow creates an A-Fold at the elbow but an X-Fold at the inside of the elbow. The same folding occurs at a bent knee.

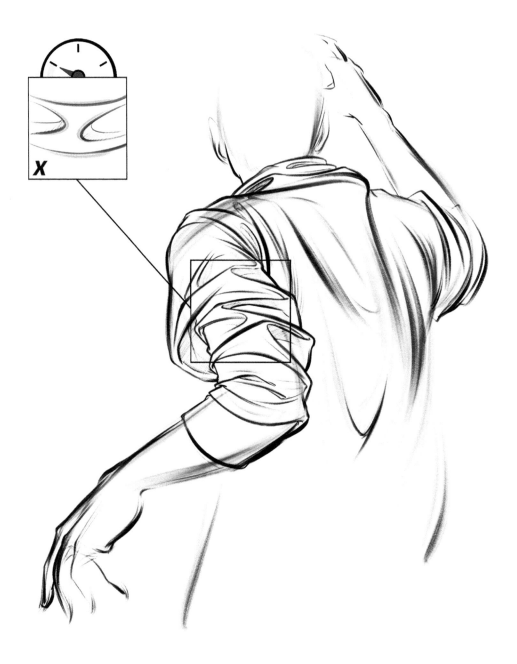

Here is another example of X-Folds where the sleeve has been pushed up to the elbow, so the X-Folds appear in the upper arm. They are slow since the apexes of the folds are very small and sharp. One challenge here is to keep the X-Folds wrapping around the arm to show form.

X-Folds are common at the bottom of jeans. The baggier the jean, the more aggressive the X-Folds. The Tension FORCES, here zigzaging around the leg, create peaks in the folds helping to form these odd pockets of structure. I also marked some the ellipses here that create clear volume.

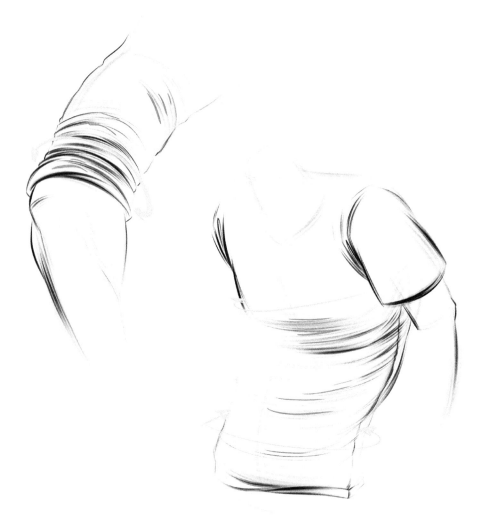

The O-Fold

The last of the fold types, The O-Fold. With the O-Fold, we stop the hang-and-flow from the prior fold types. Now, the fabric is snug to the body and heavily compressed. This creates tight rings of fabric. Athletic apparel will typically present this fold type. The O-Fold is a compressed X-Fold and occurs on tubular forms of fabric, typically on the arm, leg, and sometimes the neck.

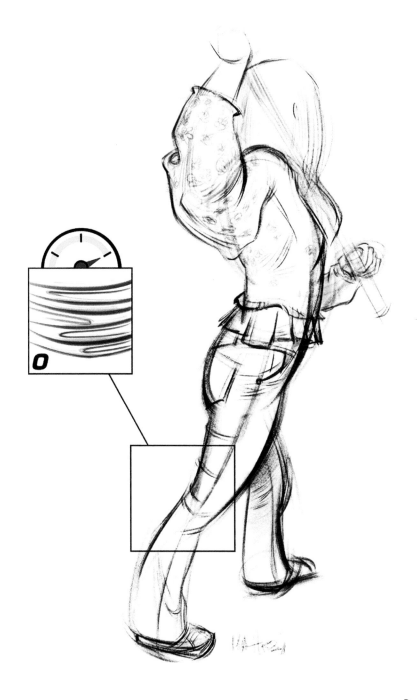

By Michael Mattesi

Jeans, probably the most ubiquitous piece of apparel, come in all different types of fits with subtle changes to the upper and lower leg width. Above we see that the tighter cut thigh shows us O-Folds across the back of Makenna's upper leg and a loose J-Fold from the back of the knee to the front of the lower leg.

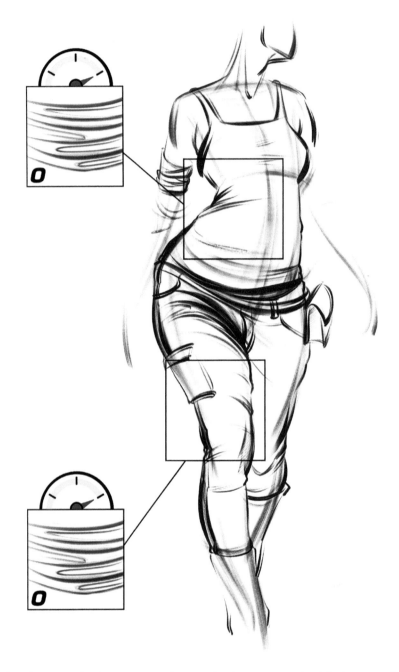

O-Folds abound with tight apparel. We can see it here in the legs, across the full distance of the tank top, and in the arm of a long sleeve shirt that has been pushed up the arm.

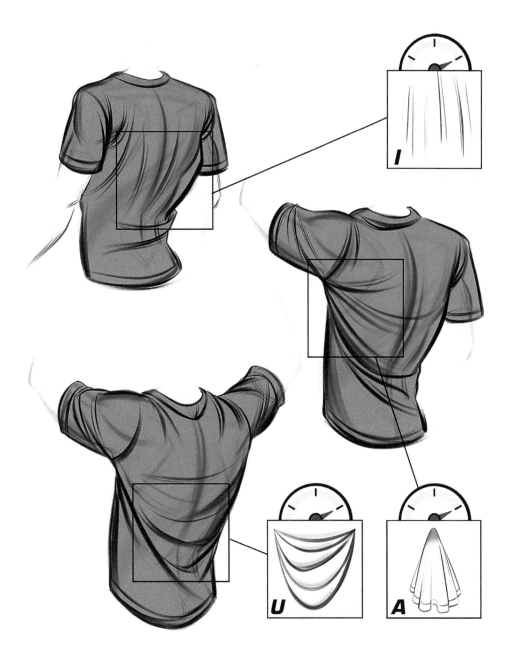

Above, we progress with I-Folds on the back which become an A-Fold as the left arm is lifted. Once both arms are raised, we move into an example of a two-point U-Fold. The fabric is thin, so all folds are fast. This page is a great example showing how the function of the boy determines the folds of his clothes.

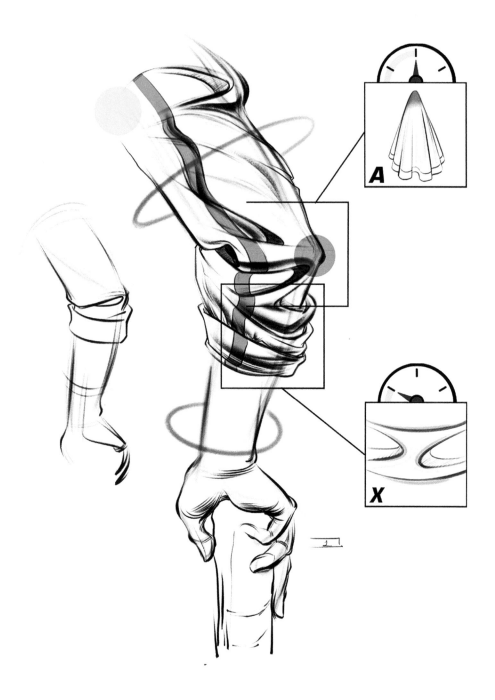

In this close-up of the arm, look at all of the information we can now discuss and illustrate. First, we want to understand that the FORCE of the arm runs down the elbow side. The purple ellipses remind us to support the forms of the arm. The Gravity and Applied FORCE Anchor Points help describe the reason behind the A-Fold. Lastly, we have the X-Folds that are compressed upward, off of the wrist, and toward the elbow.

ASSIGNMENTS

1. Learn and memorize all the fold types and the way they work!
2. Bring in your prior knowledge of Gravity and Applied Anchor points to help with the different fold types.
3. Draw on top of clothed model references to help identify the fold types found in the clothing.
4. Redraw the images found on each of the main fold type pages.
5. Draw clothed figures and identify the folds as you draw them.

BODY AND GRAVITY FORCES

Now, knowing the concept of FORCE-Fabric across FORCE, Form Shape, and Fold Types, let's move into the fit part of the book. The chapters are defined by the fit of the clothing relative to the model. Those three chapters are tight, casual, and loose-fit clothing. Why is fit significant? Fit is a strong determinant of the fabric's folds. The tighter the fit of the apparel, the more the figure's FORCES affect the fabric. The more loose the fit, the more gravity takes over.

Strength of Gravity and Applied FORCES relative to clothing fit.

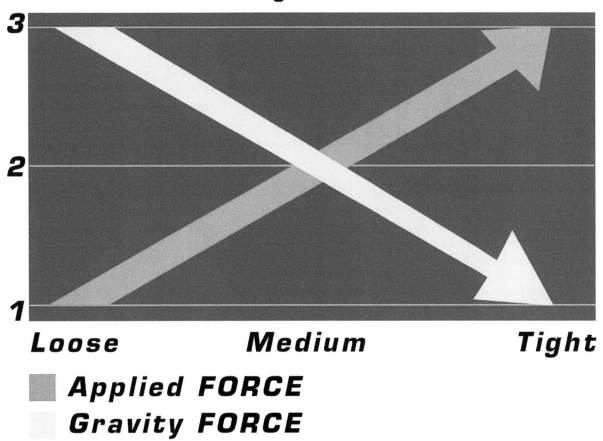

Loose   **Medium**   **Tight**

Applied FORCE
Gravity FORCE

The above chart shows how the power of Gravity FORCE, and the power of Applied FORCE relate to the fit of clothing. Gravity FORCE, in green, has a strong influence on loose-fit clothing and a weak influence on tight clothes since they don't have the opportunity to hang. The more loose the fit is, the more gravity has the opportunity to pull downward on the fabric.

Applied FORCE, in orange, is better represented in tight clothing where we can more clearly see what the body is doing.

DOI: 10.1201/9781351049467-5

TIGHT FIT

To create a system which, I believe, will help us more efficiently learn how to draw folds, I have categorized clothing fit into three categories, tight, medium, and loose fit. They are clearly marked by the three different page-edge colors for your convenience.

We start our journey on how to draw clothes with the fit that most resembles the body itself, tight-fit clothes. Since the fit is tight, it adheres to the body and therefore is most dictated by the body's FORCE instead of the gravity pulling on the fabric.

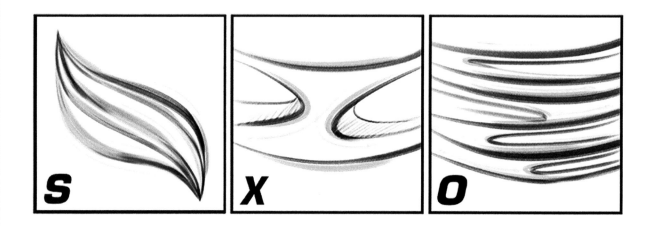

At the start of each fit type, I will present the fold-type icons that occur most in that fit type. We can make these assessments because of the rules of gravity, human anatomy, and fabric, and how they relate to one another. There is some predictability, and this will make it easier to draw clothes from reference or imagination. Most often we will find the X-Fold and when compressed the, the O-Fold. If there occurs enough of a rotation in an action of the figure, you might discover an S-Fold.

When clothes are skintight as with these pants, we do not really have folds. You may run into some O or X-Folds at the back of the knee, the top of the leg, or with the intersection of the pelvis. Look at the great seam down the center of the side of the leg. Even without folds, or detailed anatomy, which is covered by the fabric of the pants, the seams truly help us with construction.

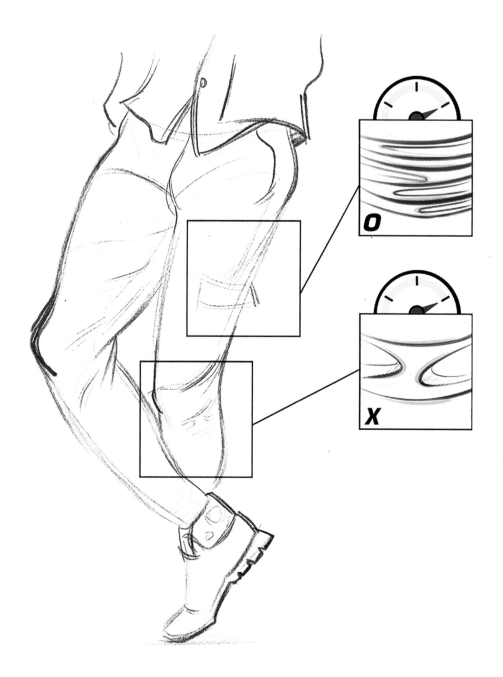

O

X

By Michael Mattesi

Above, we can see a pair of tight pants presenting I- and X-Folds. Although the I-Fold or small pipes do not hang, they pull from separate anchor points from the seam of the pants' leg and across the inner leg and thigh. Below the model's left leg, we find a small occurrence of the X-Fold bunching up under the knee and above the calf.

Wow, what a great example of tight-fit clothes. The seam down the side of the model is full of O-Folds that help us comprehend a sense of how smooth the texture of the fabric must be. All the folds her wrap around the model's form sharing with us the different orientations in space her ribcage and pelvis occupy.

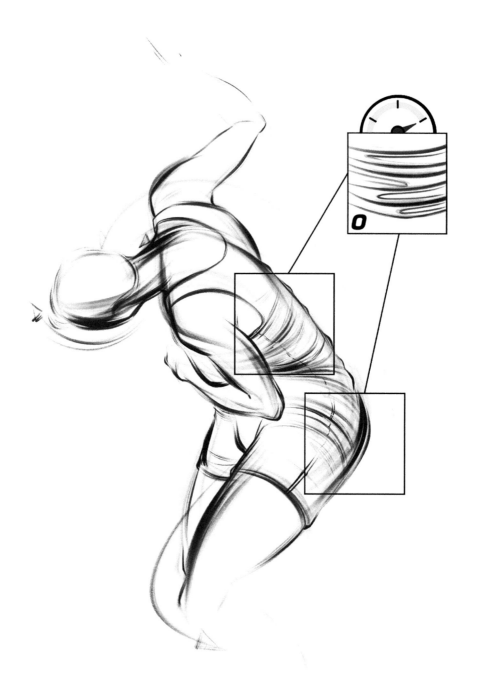

Here, tight-fit clothing clings to the body in stretched tight O-shaped folds, which really help us to see the clear ellipses in the body. The O-Folds and compressed X-Folds are form-revealing and present the direction of the upper leg and rib cage in space.

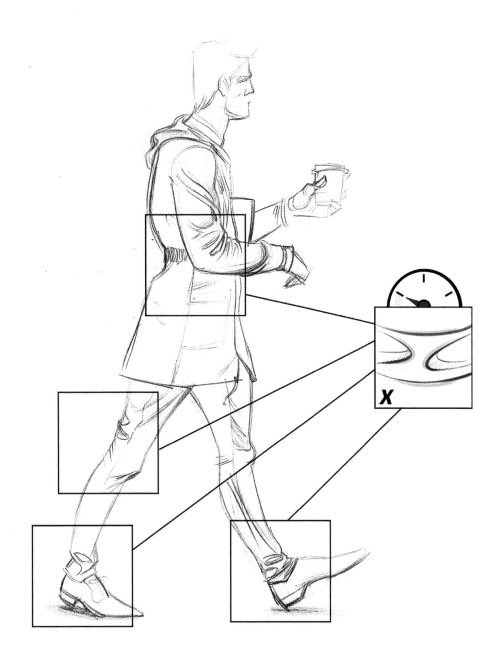

By Michael Mattesi

These tight garments present numerous X-Fold moments found in the jacket and the slim fit pants. The tapered leg allows for enough fabric for a few X-Folds to occur while the pants sit on top of the shoes. This drawing was done on location

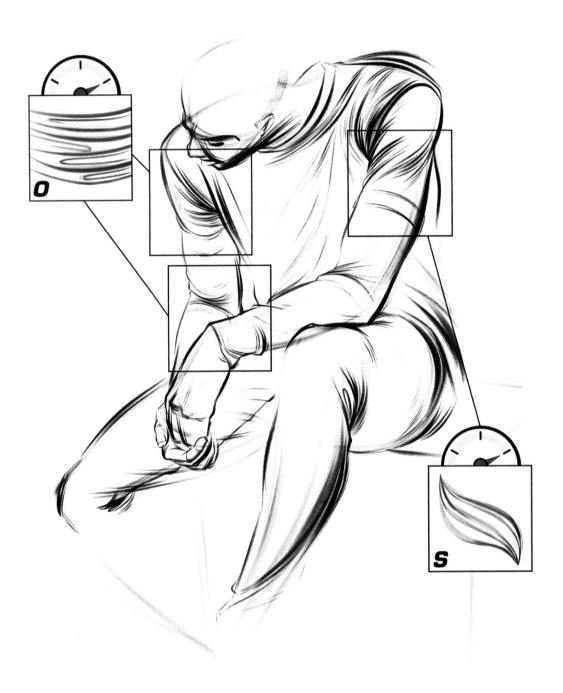

Tight garments can present more than O- and X-Folds. This fluid and snug fitting top shows an S-Fold hiding pulling of the shoulder and gracefully wrapping itself around the deltoid of the arm. The subtle indent of the deltoid helps create this opportunity for the S-Fold to occur. If the shirt was medium or loose fit, the fabric would hand more in a J-Fold from the back of the shoulder and then hook on and around the elbow.

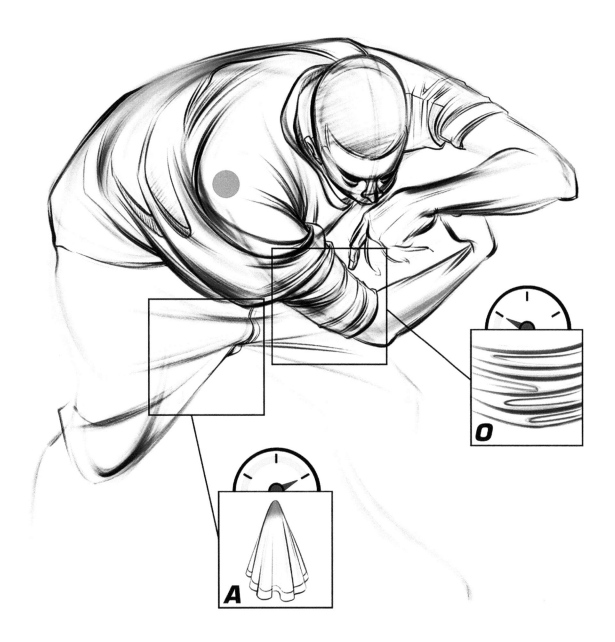

We can see the O-Folds in the arm, and some great, bold A-Folds emanating from the seam in the crotch. I enjoy the contrast of folds, here, from tight to very loose. Notice how the rest of the shirt is relatively loose as well.

ASSIGNMENTS

1. Find clothed model reference with loose-fit clothing.

2. Draw Gravity and Applied FORCE Anchor Points on the photo reference.

3. Draw over, and identify, the different fold types.

4. Now, go draw your figure. Start with an unclothed model drawing to find FORCE Shapes, rhythm, and forms.

5. Draw the clothing on top of the figure drawing.

6. After this practice, draw the clothed model, from the start, with study on the clothing and the folds that best show function and form!

7. Then, with much experience, draw figures from imagination, and clothe them as well.

MEDIUM FIT

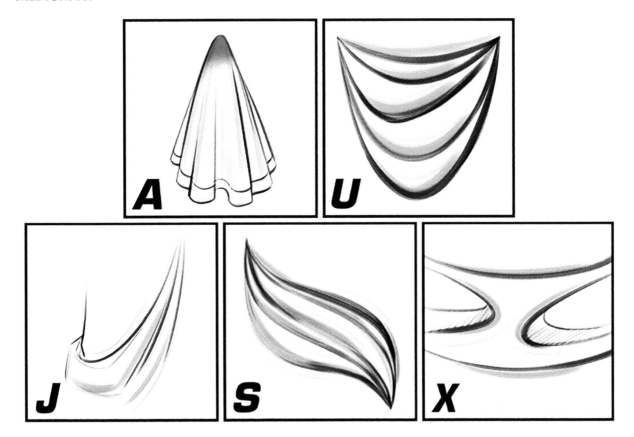

Notice how some folds go against the concept of form. Curves could realistically go against the form of the arm. Using hierarchy, find folds that help present the correct form/direction in space, of the area of the body. Medium fit finds a place where the clothes are not as tight a fit as the prior chapter, so Gravity FORCE begins to play a part in the hanging of the fabric, and is also affected by the FORCES of the figure. For most of us, this is the fit of clothing we most commonly wear.

By Michael Mattesi

Looking at poses of athletes practicing Kav Maga, a military self-defense and fighting system developed for the Israeli Defense FORCES (IDF) derived from a combination of techniques sourced from boxing, wrestling, aikido, judo, and karate, along with realistic fight training, I drew their medium-fit clothing. So, we can see the effects of the body's and gravity's FORCES. Many A type Folds pull from the model's right shoulder creating rays across the back of the model. In the back of the right knee, we find X-Folds since the leg is such a cylinder and with compression caused back the bent joint, the tube compresses creating those X-Folds. Stay aware of how to edit the folds. It is easy to draw folds that confuse the form of the area of the body you are drawing.

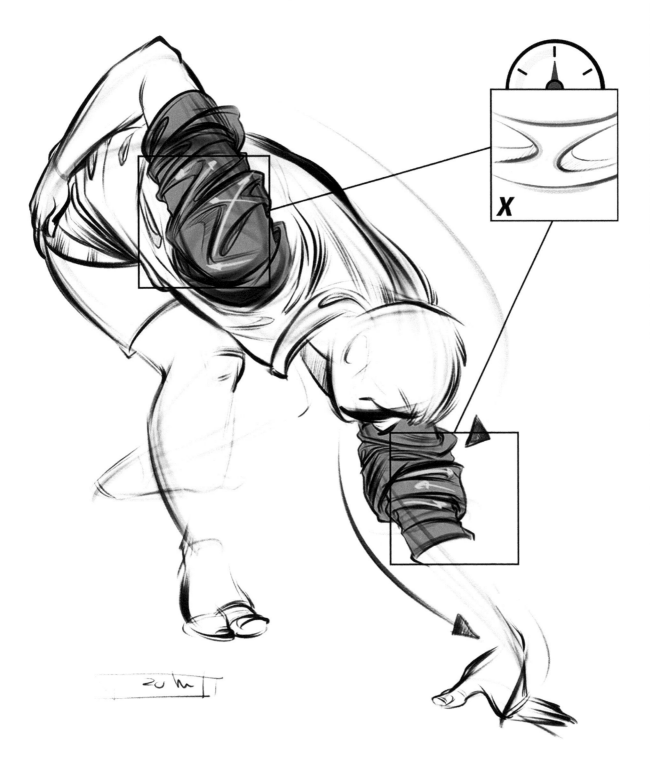

This drawing further presents the importance of using the correct fold in which to inform the volume of the area of the body being drawn. Notice the use of the X-FOLD around the closer arm. If the fabric had been a slightly tighter fit, this would have been the O-FOLD. From the model's right shoulder to left hip, we find an excellent example of a J-Fold. It hangs from the shoulder and dives down the back to finally hook itself, and over the left side of the body.

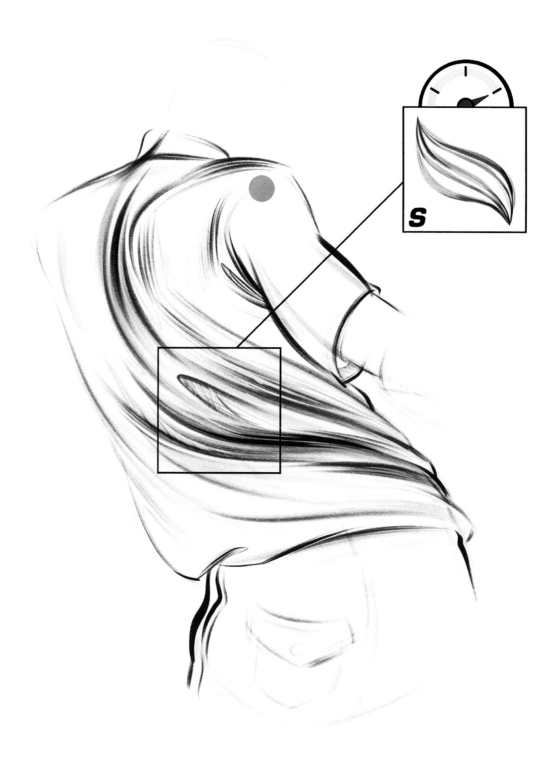

Just loose enough, here the folds pull across the back from the Gravity Anchor Point at the shoulder to the Applied FORCE Anchor Point in the hip. These folds do a great job of clarifying the S rhythm of the torso and are created because of the body's rhythm.

Keeping to the subject of shirts, look at this slightly, more loose-fitting shirt, and notice the X-Folds again showing up in the sleeves. Initial anchor points usually start the fold path downward from the shoulders.

In this last drawing, with a focus on the arms, look at the X-Folds compress upon one another as the sleeves are pressed up to the shoulders, shortening the length of the sleeves, and folding the pliable fabric.

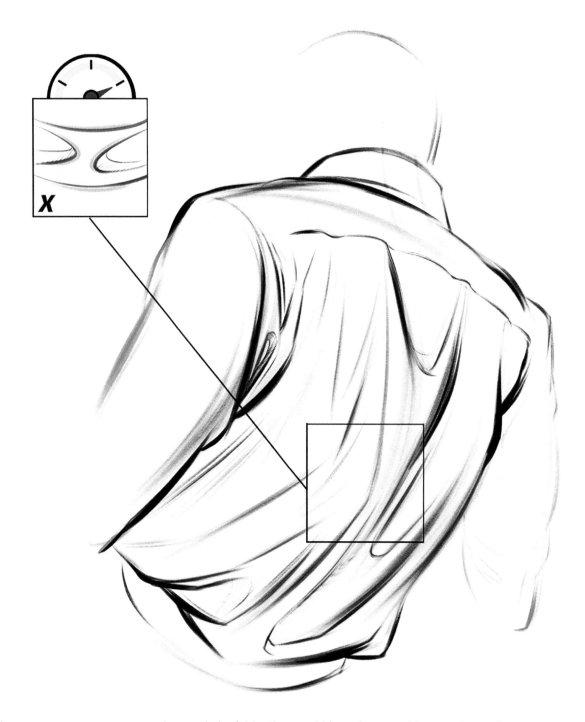

There is an interesting scenario here with the folds. They could have been I-Folds since the anchor points move from the top to the bottom of the back, but instead, we have something of a very wide X-Fold present here. I think this is due to the left-to-right compression across the back, instead of only the hanging on the back caused by gravity.

Here, once again, we find the X-Fold move numerous times across the front of the torso due to compression caused by the bend between the ribcage and pelvis. The anchor points for these folds reside on the far left and right sides of the torso. See if you can find all of these moments in the drawing.

The A-Fold Anchor Point in the arm pit is the starting point of the folds which radiate out across the back. Near the arm pit, once again, fabric pulls down and around the upper arm, in a J-Fold, as it hooks around the bicep. Both of these folds hang from a Gravity Anchor Point in the shoulder.

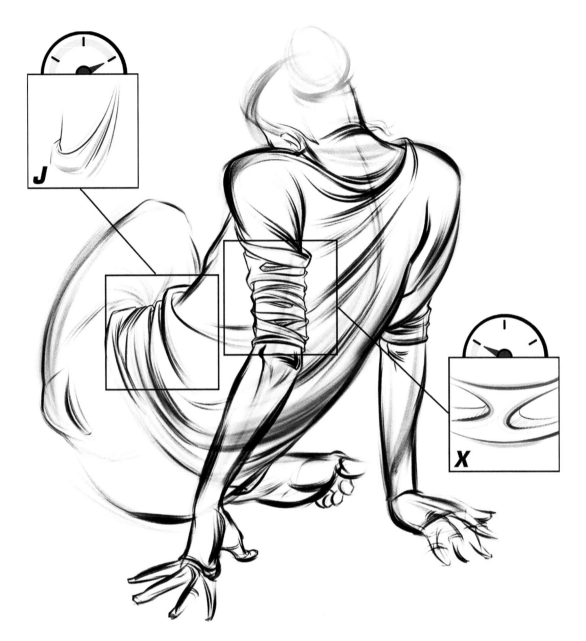

Check out the X-Folds on the model's left arm, floating over the J-Folds that stretch from the Gravity Anchor Point at the right shoulder, and move under the arm hooking around the left side of the ribcage. With medium-fit clothes, you can see there is quite a variety of folds. We don't find the O-Fold since the clothing is not tight enough to do so.

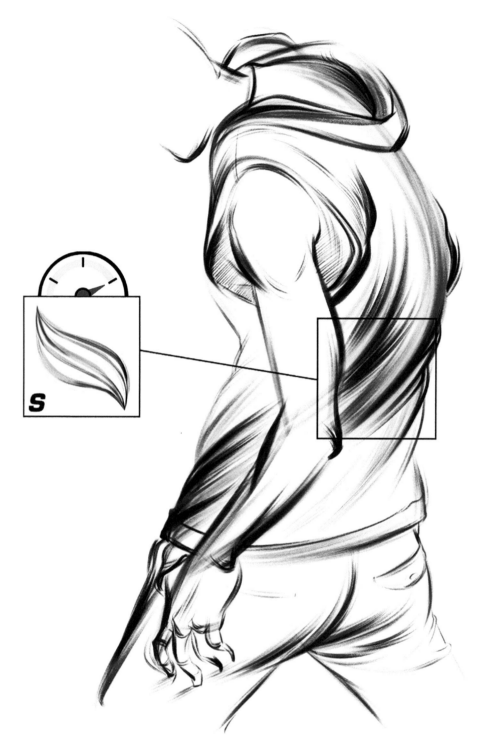

Here is another S-Fold running across the back in the opposite direction of the one we discussed a few pages back. Once again, it presents the rhythm of the torso with clarity and grace. Do keep in mind that the folds contain thickness and form. These folds are high speed since they are very open with no tight curves.

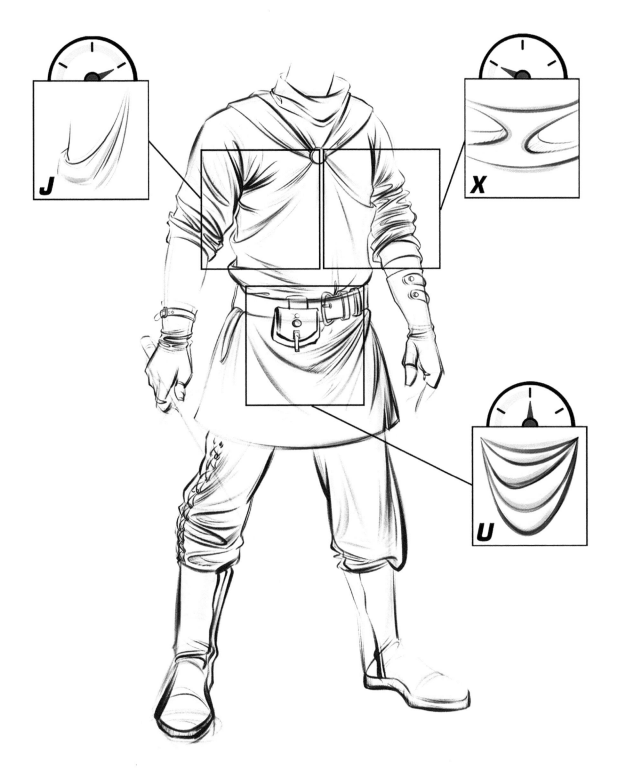

Here, we find an outfit that presents folds of three different speeds. At the top left corner, we find fast, FORCE-Fabric in a J-Fold. In the top right corner, the X-Fold, with very tight curves, is considered a slow fold. Below the belt, we have the U-Fold hanging from each side of the pelvis. The U-Folds are medium in speed due to the somewhat angular cornering in the drop of the folds. If they had been a touch more open, we could have pushed the speedometer up to fast. See the other clear X-Folds, not marked in the image, in the leg on the left side of the page.

This S-Fold is more unique than the others because it presents the rarest torso template of the human figure, the Reverse S Torso. The Reverse S moves from the chest and moves across the body to the back of the pelvis. This is called a Reverse S because the natural S rhythm of the torso, in the side view moves from the back across to the stomach. These folds are fast as they flow across the torso.

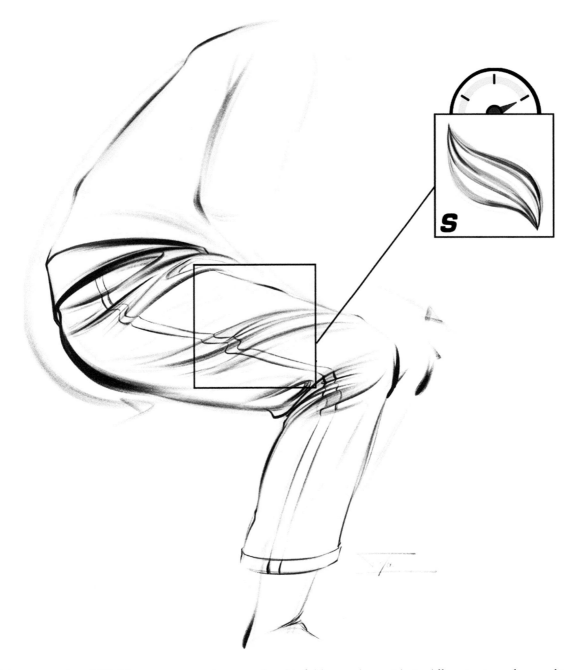

We've seen a lot of S-Folds move across the torso, but this fold can also reside in different areas of an outfit, and we can witness that above. On the side of the leg, we pull from the bottom of the pelvis and diagonally across, up to the front of the thigh.

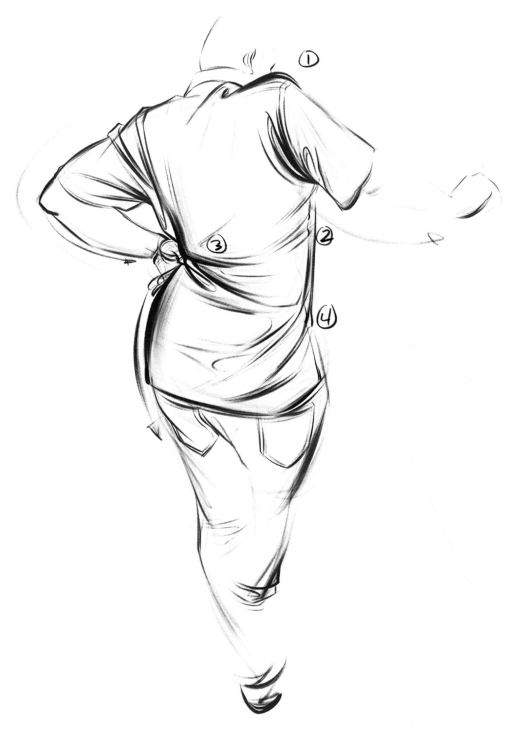

Each of the numbers above represents an area with folds in the fabric. Take a moment and see if you can identify the fold types. Look at how many anchor points there are, and at the general shape of the fold area. Why are the folds being generated? To find the answers, look to the next page.

ASSIGNMENTS

1. Find clothed model reference with loose-fit clothing.

2. Draw Gravity and Applied FORCE Anchor Points on the photo reference.

3. Draw over, and identify, the different fold types.

4. Now go draw you figure. Start with an unclothed model, drawing to find FORCE Shapes, rhythm, and forms.

5. Draw the clothing on top of the figure drawing.

6. After this practice, draw the clothed model, from the start, with study on the clothing and the folds that best show function and form!

7. Then, with much experience, draw figures from imagination and clothe them as well.

Answers to assignment questions:

1. A
2. O
3. A
4. A

LOOSE-FIT APPAREL

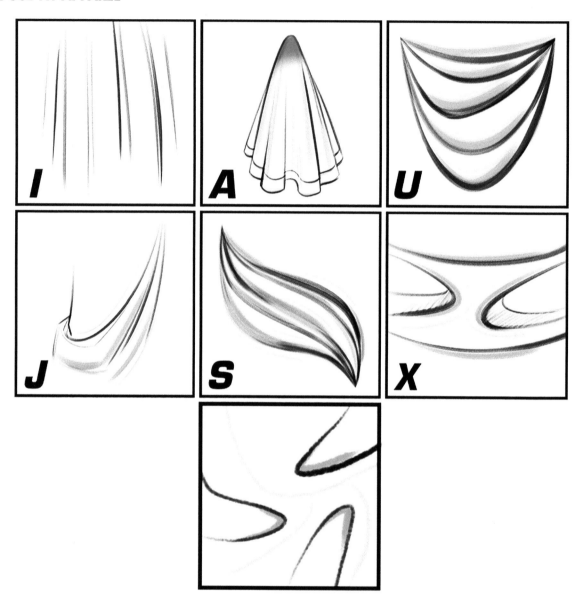

In this chapter, we discuss the Loose Fit. We will analyze clothes that are mostly controlled by the FORCE of gravity. Different fabric types are most easily understood in loose clothes since the fabric hangs, and the sharpness of the fold corners shows how hard or soft a fabric is.

In fashion, the concept of clothing hanging, due to gravity, is called draping. In fact, draping muslin, a cheap cotton fabric, on top of a mannequin, is where the first step of draping begins. The muslin pieces are refined on the mannequin and then removed. The patterns for the apparel are further refined and put on a mannequin again once more. They are repeatedly further iterated until they are ready to place on a real model. Below is a more high-level list of the general process:

1. Conceptualization: The designer will come up with an idea for the piece of apparel, taking into account current fashion trends, consumer preferences, and their own design aesthetic.

2. Sketching: The designer will create sketches of the piece of apparel, experimenting with different designs and details.

3. Selection of fabrics: The designer will choose the fabrics that will be used for the piece of apparel, taking into account factors such as durability, comfort, and drape.

4. Pattern making: The designer will create a pattern for the piece of apparel, using the sketches and fabric choices as a guide.

5. Fitting and adjustments: The designer will create a prototype of the piece of appare, land make any necessary adjustments to ensure a good fit.

6. Sampling: The designer will create a sample of the piece of apparel to show to potential buyers or to test its wearability and durability.

7. Production: Once the design is finalized, the piece of apparel will be produced in large quantities to be sold to consumers.

8. Marketing and distribution: The apparel is then marketed and distributed to the target market through different channels, such as retail stores, e-commerce, wholesale, or others.

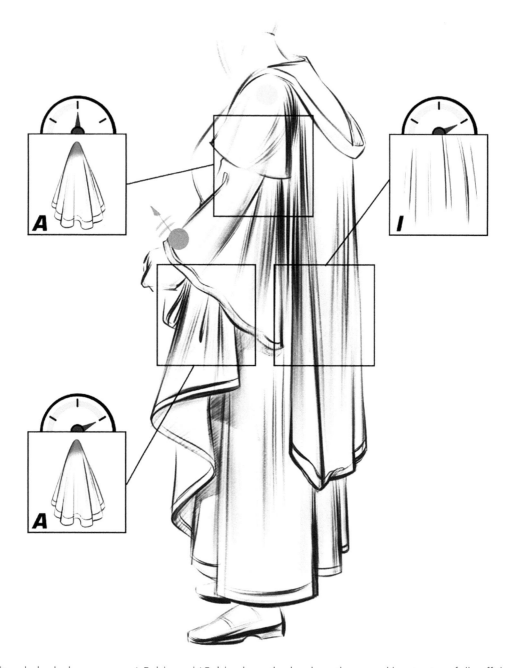

This medieval cloak shows many A-Folds and I-Folds along the back as the cape-like structure falls off the back and downward. Gravity, once again pulls the fabric toward the ground. The top left A-Fold Anchor Point sits behind the arm hidden as the radiating lines fall down to the edge of the cuff.

Now, we find the introduction of the J-Fold in Loose-Fit Clothing. Remember the J-Fold is an A-Fold with a hook on the end that wraps around a form of the body. Many U-Folds occur from the two Gravity Points, the hip and the bunched fabric in the hand.

Here is an excellent toga expressing three different folds, the J-, A-, and I-Folds. Notice how the pin in the chest creates the Gravity Anchor Point for the A-Fold. The I-Folds fall from the Gravity Anchor Points of the belt line. The massive J-Fold pulls from the Gravity Anchor Point at the hip and pulls and falls down around the front of the body and around the closer leg.

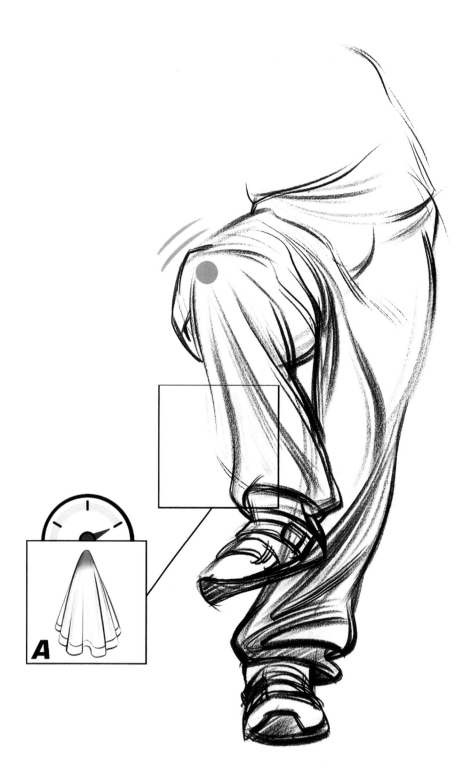

The clear A-Fold is caused by an Applied Anchor Point at the knee, and the folds fall down around the ankle and over the foot.

Fabric collects at the right arm's inner elbow, and creates a couple of A-Folds that pull to the left. Uniquely, we flow into the inner elbow from the shoulder with an S-Fold! Pay attention to those anchor points to understand the twist in the arm that creates these different folds.

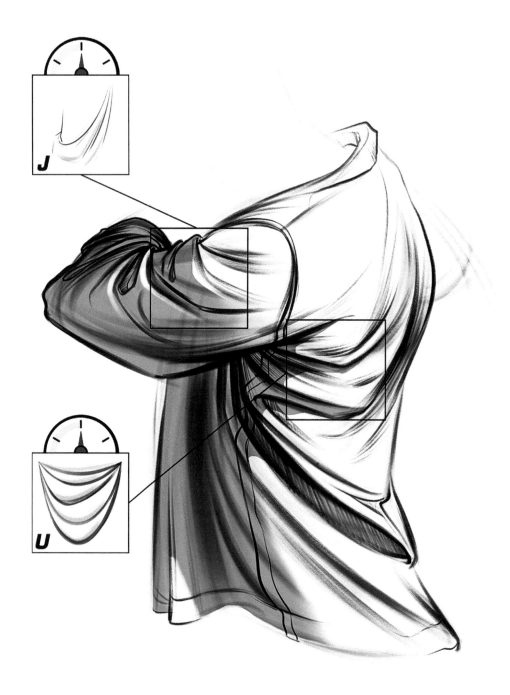

Here is a group of massive U-Folds that connect from the far-right shoulder to the arm pit of the left arm. In the left sleeve, we see the J-Fold wrap its way around the structure of the deltoid and hook over the top edge of the arm. The J-Fold comes from the Gravity Anchor Point in the shoulder and then moves to the Applied FORCE Anchor Point on the bicep side of the arm. As some extra flair, Mritunjay rendered the drawing to show how successful these folds are in creating FORCES and forms of the figure.

The fast J-Folds in the arm hang once more, from the shoulder and hook around the lower arm at the wrist. Some big X-Folds collapse around the knees in big half speed folds.

A

X

A-Folds drop from the shoulder and do not become the J-Fold, but instead, crumple up at the inner elbow into some medium speed X-Folds. Discuss different colors for the anchor point between the sticker and the art

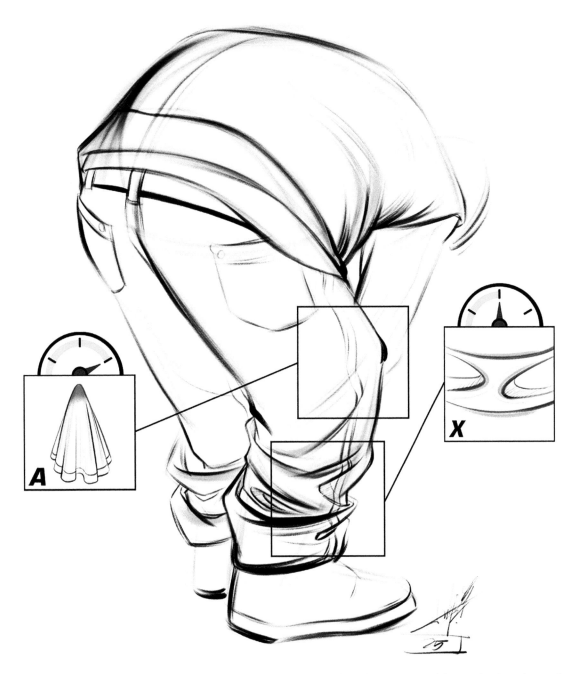

Similar to the last image, we run through the same exact system of the hanging A-Folds into the bunching of X-Folds. In this case, the knee and the ankle create the same effect as the elbow in the last image. So, one common system we have learned thus far is the A-Fold can be on its own, become a J-Fold, or an X-Fold!

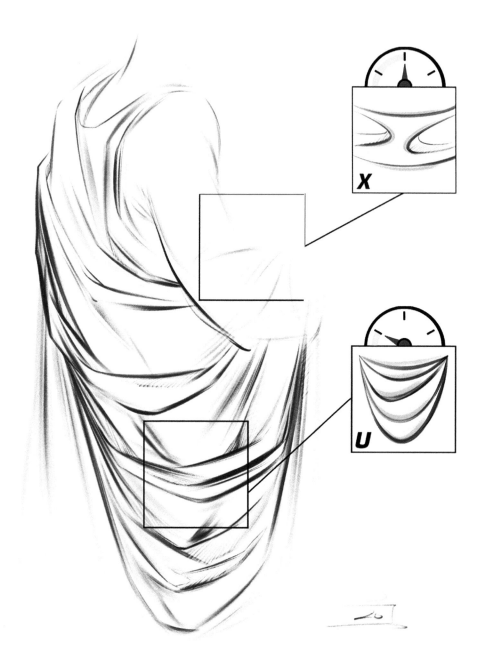

The X-Folds here are opposite the A-Fold created by Applied FORCE in the elbow. Below the arm, we experience a very dramatic series of U-Folds that hang from an Applied FORCE Anchor Point, behind the arm, to the Gravity Anchor Point that would be found on the model's left shoulder. Since the U-Folds have hard corners, I have labeled the folds slow speed.

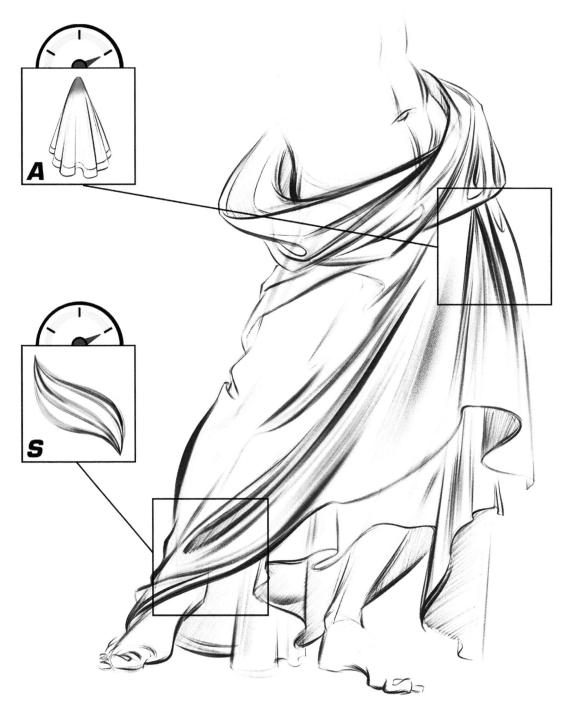

Talk about loose drapery, we have a dramatic A-Fold hanging from the hip that later feeds and S-Fold, versus a more unique combination of the A to J or the A to X-Folds. Notice the massive ellipse found at the waist as well, which helps the torso emerge out of the pelvis and lean toward the camera.

Why is that not an A-Fold? There are numerous anchor points at both ends of the I-Folds seen stretching across the model's back in this dramatic pose. Another observation, while not highlighted here, is the A-Fold set up at the knee. The front of the knee is the Applied FORCE Anchor Point, and the folds pull down around the back of the leg. They could become X- or O-Folds at that point depending on the tightness of the leg bend and/or the thickness of the fabric

A beautiful S-Fold loops up from the elbow here and around the forearm caused by the ninety-degree rotation of the wrist. This S-Fold is close to being a J-Fold. The reason it is not is because we can see that the fold continues on its way to the hand. If the fold had been more of a hook, it would have been classified as the J-Fold.

The J-Fold here is close to becoming an A-Fold. It's not because the A-Fold has a single point that tension folds pull from. Here, there many Applied FORCE anchor points which could make this an I-Fold, but since they hook around the arm, what we have are multiple J-Folds. On the left side of the drawing, we see numerous I-Folds falling from the hand that clasp the fabric.

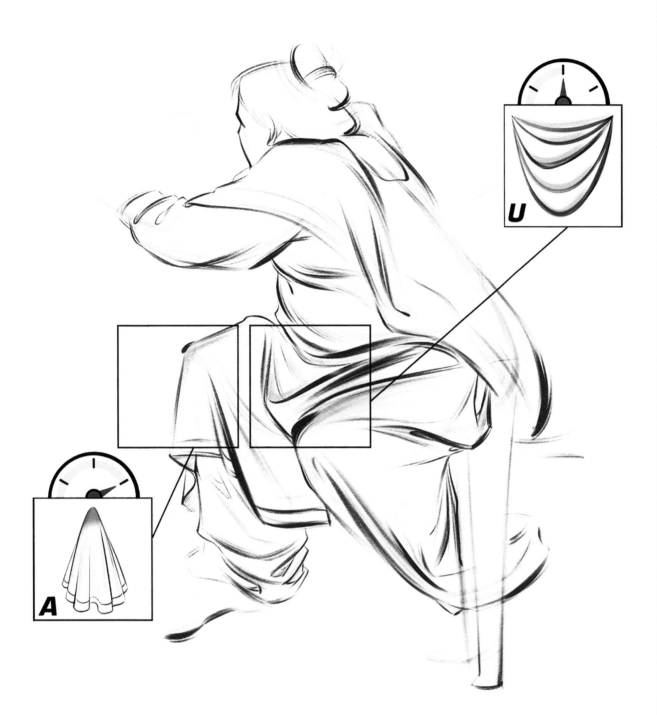

In our final drawing on loose-fit clothes, we witness A- and U-Folds clearly represented through the team of function, presentation of the body, and gravity. The speed of each of these folds is relatively fast since the peaks of the folds are not pinched.

ASSIGNMENTS

1. Find clothed model reference with loose-fit clothing.

2. Draw Gravity and Applied FORCE Anchor Points on the photo reference.

3. Draw over, and identify, the different fold types.

4. Now go draw you figure. Start with an unclothed model, drawing to find FORCE Shapes, rhythm, and forms.

5. Draw the clothing on top of the figure drawing.

6. After this practice, draw the clothed model, from the start, with study on the clothing and the folds that best show function and form!

7. Then, with much experience, draw figures from imagination and clothe them as well.

Now, for this part of the book, we are going to discuss some different processes that will help you learn to draw clothing on figures. A great place to start is to use photos of models. This is similar to the old-school paper doll concept, except you are going to draw the clothes. I suggest you find an outfit you like from the internet or a clothing catalog. Once you have chosen the model photo, find the different anchor points on the model. What's interesting to note here, is that the shoulder has two anchor points, one Gravity and one Applied FORCE. The Gravity Anchor Point establishes the arm allowing the elbow to take on the role of the Applied FORCE Anchor Point. Then, there is the Applied FORCE Anchor Point in the shoulder that pulls from the Gravity FORCE Anchor Point in the hip. Let's see how that plays out when we dress Trinda.

DOI: 10.1201/9781351049467-6

We are going to start with a tight clothing fit. Let's primarily focus on finding the Applied FORCE Anchor Points. The pose presents torque, rotation, and much foreshortening. Look at the arm. The right shoulder is a Gravity Anchor Point for the right arm and the elbow is an Applied FORCE Anchor Point. That same shoulder is an Applied FORCE Anchor Point for the torso as it pulls the figure forward through the rotation. The right hip is the Gravity Anchor Point in this relationship between those two points.

Since we know the location of the different anchor points based on the function of gravity and the model's FORCES, we can now apply a medium-fit outfit and clothe Trinda, the model. With a fit that is slightly more loose, folds could change from O-Folds to X-Folds. Others, like A-Folds, can now be clearer and more exaggerated.

With this loose, toga-like outfit, we can most clearly see some of the folds from the prior fit, such as the A-Fold of the forward knee, and some new folds emerging, like the S-Folds that connect the two legs.

Here is another model photo with a medium-fit outfit. Notice the different fold types and the similarities to the Trinda poses. Spend some time doing many of these overlays, and learn to go from choosing an outfit to dressing a model with it. Learn how to identify, and use, the anchor points to connect them with Tension FORCES. Keep in mind the type of fabric, because it will determine the speed of the folds.

DrawingFORCE.com

By Michael Mattesi

Here, I dress Trinda in a snug fitting Bond like suit. Most of the pull in this suit comes from the Applied FORCE Anchor Point of the shoulder in the raised arm. The pants also pull from the crotch to the forward bent knee. The suit is loose enough to dodge any O-Folds and tight enough to stay with mostly A-Folds.

By Michael Mattesi

Noe wears wide-leg pants and a cropped top with long sleeve outfit. The pants were fun to draw here with their hanging moments off her pelvis and each leg. Here we have some A-Folds, J-Folds, and S-Folds.

Now, let's see if we can dress a FORCE figure drawing. I chose one from the front of the book to reintroduce us to the model's Directional and Applied FORCES. See the upward thrust of the model's right shoulder and the outstretched, raised right arm.

In preparing the drawing for the outfit, I called out the main orientations of the forms with the purple ellipses. I added a few Gravity and Applied FORCE Anchor Points. Extended from those points, I drew Tension FORCE lines to prepare for the folds.

Here is the outfit, a medium-fit tunic top and pants with a loose-fit tail. Notice how all the preparation helped bring the pre-existing ideas from our FORCE figure drawing to dressing the model. The Gravity Anchor Points around the waist made it simple to illustrate draped fabric here. The systems of the right arm clearly set up how the tunic was drawn here.

Let's go through the process again. The first step again is to draw your FORCE figure, if from reference or imagination. Use FORCE, Form, and Shape to do so. In this initial drawing, observe how Mritunjay implied form at numerous points, the pelvis, and around the ribcage.

Using the tools learned in the book, think about the type of fabric you are using for the model's clothing. Then, identify the shape of the patterns, the seams they create and what type of silhouette they make on the figure. Now, very important, find the Applied and Gravity Anchor Points. Once they are established, draw the fold lines based on how the Tension FORCES move around the body, the FORCES of the pose, fabric type, fit, and FORCE of Gravity.

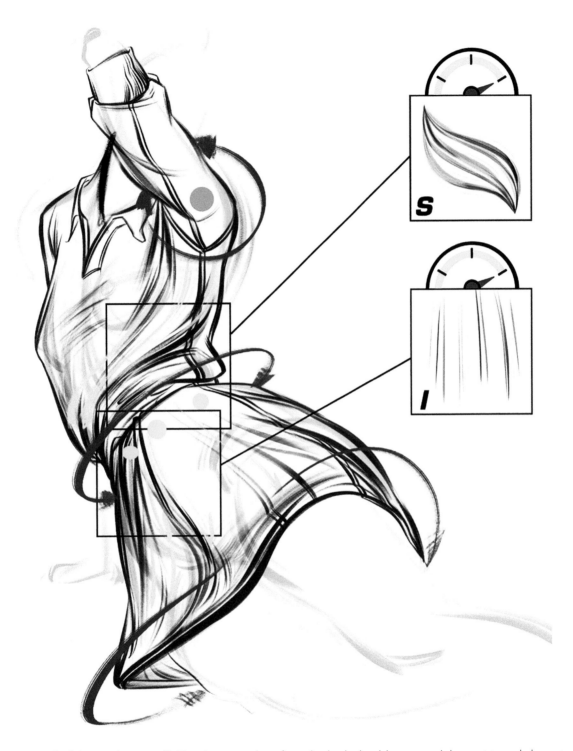

S

I

Once more, all of the work pays off. The dramatic drop from the high shoulder, around the waist, and down to the far hip, defines a strong S-Fold across the ribs. The top of the skirt defines clear form. The Gravity Anchor Points allow the Tension FORCES to outwardly flow from gathered points to the ends of the skirt. The seams down the center of the side of her top and skirt further define the forms.

This is, again, a drawing from the beginning of the book. Use those body FORCES to get you started with the anchor points and Tension FORCES.

Here, I placed an Applied FORCE Anchor Point in the right shoulder since it's driving upward. There is also a Gravity Anchor Point in the seam of the crotch. Let the Tension FORCES flow. They run down the right and middle of the back. On the right leg, they pull from the crotch to the outside edge of the ankle. Keep in mind, the right side of the thigh is where the fabric would hang from.

This is our last process drawing before we move onto the last chapter of the book, Texture. We now have the clothed model, and a representation of everything we have learned up to now about working with fabric on figure drawings that were not previously clothed!

TEXTURE

In our last chapter on Folds and drawing clothes, we're going to discuss the icing on the cake, texture. Yes, we can indicate the texture of clothes with line! I don't mean cross hatching or stippling. Think of line having nine basic variations. They start with the thickness of the line, then the straightness to curvature and rhythmic fluidity of the line, and the opacity which you control with pressure.

1. Thin width, angular with either light, medium, or dark opacity.

2. Medium width, curved with either light, medium, or dark opacity.

3. Wide width, rhythmic with either light, medium, or dark opacity.

Texture brings much contrast and character to drawings. The great fashion illustrators from the 1950s to the 1970s skillfully illustrated line art which was used for ads in newspapers and magazines around the world. Check out the following list of amazing fashion illustrators:

1. Rene Gruau: A French illustrator who was known for his elegant and stylish illustrations of fashion and beauty. He worked for many of the most famous fashion houses of the 20th century, including Dior, Schiaparelli, and Balenciaga.

2. Joe Eula: An American fashion illustrator who was known for his bold and colorful drawings of fashion and beauty. He worked for many of the most famous fashion magazines and brands of the 20th century, including Vogue, Harper's Bazaar, and Estée Lauder.

3. David Downton: A British illustrator who is known for his elegant and detailed illustrations of fashion and beauty. He has worked for many of the most famous fashion houses and magazines of the 21st century, including Vogue, Harper's Bazaar, and Dior.

4. Robert Best: An American illustrator who was known for his bold and colorful illustrations of fashion, beauty, and celebrities. He worked for many of the most famous fashion magazines and brands of the time, including Harper's Bazaar, Vogue, and Revlon.

5. Rene Bouché: An American illustrator who was known for his elegant and sophisticated illustrations of fashion, beauty, and celebrities. He worked for many of the most famous fashion magazines and brands of the time, including Harper's Bazaar, Vogue, and Coco Chanel.

Unfortunately, the use of fashion illustration in advertising declined in the late 1990s due to photography, the internet, and more video instead of still images. The cost of photography was also less than hiring an illustrator. However, it's worth noting that fashion illustration is still used in some specific areas such as luxury brands, editorial media, and in some cases, for commercial projects. It is considered an art form and a means of expressing the designer's vision. It has a timeless quality to it that many people still appreciate.

Different fabrics have different attributes that can affect their look and feel, as well as their suitability for certain garments or styles. Some of the most common fabric attributes include

- Fiber type: The type of fiber used to make a fabric can affect its characteristics, such as its strength, drape, and durability. Common types of fibers include cotton, linen, silk, wool, polyester, and nylon.

DOI: 10.1201/9781351049467-7

- Weave: The way the fibers are woven together can affect the fabric's appearance and properties, such as its texture, drape, and durability. Common types of weaves include plain, twill, satin, and jacquard.

- Weight: The weight of a fabric affects its drape and how it falls on the body. Lightweight fabrics, such as chiffon or georgette, tend to drape and flow, while heavier fabrics, like denim or wool, tend to hold their shape.

- Stretch: Some fabrics have a certain amount of stretch, which affect the fit and comfort of a garment. Stretch fabrics, such as spandex or lycra, are often used in form-fitting garments.

- Transparency: Some fabrics are more transparent than others and may apply a specific suitability to a garment for certain occasions or settings. Transparent fabrics, such as chiffon or sheer lace, may require lining or layering to be worn in public.

Here are some of the most common fabrics that today's clothes are made from:

- Cotton: Cotton is a natural, breathable fiber that is soft, absorbent, and durable. Cotton fabrics are comfortable to wear and easy to care for, but they tend to wrinkle easily.

- Linen: Linen is a natural, breathable fiber that is strong, absorbent, and durable. Linen fabrics are cool and comfortable to wear, but they tend to wrinkle easily and require ironing.

- Silk: Silk is a natural, lustrous fiber that is soft, strong, and absorbent. Silk fabrics drape well and have a luxurious feel, but they tend to be delicate and require special care.

- Wool: Wool is a natural, warm, and insulating fiber that is soft, strong, and absorbent. Wool fabrics are comfortable to wear and easy to care for, but they can be itchy and tend to shrink when washed.

- Polyester: Polyester is a synthetic fiber that is strong, durable, and wrinkle-resistant. Polyester fabrics are easy to care for, but they tend to be less breathable than natural fibers.

- Nylon: Nylon is a synthetic fiber that is strong, durable, and wrinkle-resistant. Nylon fabrics are easy to care for, but they tend to be less breathable than natural fibers.

- Leathers: Leather is a strong and durable material that can last for many years if well maintained. Leather is a flexible material that molds to the shape of the body, making it comfortable to wear. There are different types of leather based on the tanning process, for example: full-grain leather, top-grain leather, genuine leather, corrected-grain leather, and bonded leather.

All drawings in this chapter are drawn by me, except for one awesome illustration by Mritunjay. Now let's take everything we have learned in this book and bring it to the last set of drawings.

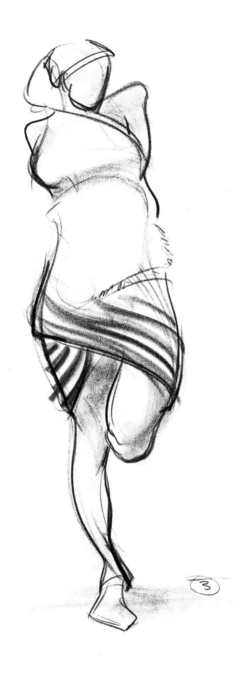

By Michael Mattesi

Let's start off really simple. There are two textures found in this outfit, smooth silk like material and a piece of short-haired fur wrapped around the model's waistline. See the importance of the fabric's contour to share that texture information. There are small notes of hairy on the drawings right side above the model's hip and those types of hairy lines also show up at the bottom of that fabric and the top left corner. These small hints show us the feel of the fabric and that it is different from the silky-smooth fabric that hugs the model's body.

Contrast in art creates visual interest, and here, the most obvious contrast lies between the thick, dark, strongly curved lines of the tight jeans on the model's thighs and the soft and loose shirt that hangs from her arm. You'll also see the stiffness of the hat and the tough, angularity of the shoes.

By Michael Mattesi

This five-minute drawing shows us the stiff, woven texture of the hat's trim against the feathery trim of this coat. That soft edge contrasts, once more, against the tight jeans and hard thighs of the model.

By Michael Mattesi

The nude figure, itself, has a few textures which need to be addressed before we deal with the fabric that clothes the model. The three key textures of the body are muscle, bone, and hair. We have seen two examples now of how the flexed muscle of the model's leg helped created hard textures. In this drawing, look at the softness of the model's hair against the bone of the elbow pushing outward against the shirt he wears. So, although the shirt's fabric is soft, and we can see this as it hangs from his shoulders down to his waist, his anatomy presents a hard texture.

By Michael Mattesi

My daughter Marin wears a cotton, coal parka. Its stiff fabric keeps the length of the upper and lower arm without folds until the fabric needs to break at the elbow. Observe how the pocket fits the center of the shape between the front opening of the jacket and the side seam.

By Michael Mattesi

I enjoy the thick leathery line we see here in the boot. It is different from the thinner lines used to describe the fluid fabric of the flowy shirt. The brim of the hat on the other hand is stiff and perfect.

By Michael Mattesi

In all of these drawings, the model wears a heavy, and yet flexible, shawl that is defined by its ability to cling to the shoulders and drape so directly from the model's contours. These folds are clear I-Folds created by gravity.

By Michael Mattesi

The randomness of the folds in this three-tiered, ruffled dress offered a great opportunity for depicting texture. I enjoy the contrast between those ruffles and the smooth, fluid line used to represent the fabric of the clingy top.

By Michael Mattesi

The addition of color helps separate fabrics and texture. The red leather bolero top and leather pants call for a relaxed line that is different from the texture presented by the black line. The black line is saved for the harder and more structured fabric of the corset, and the tougher leather shoes.

By Michael Mattesi

This cotton-only, crinkled, raw-edged, ruffled dress by H&M shows great contrast between the snug, smooth top, and the rough and jagged silhouette of the bottom portion of the dress.

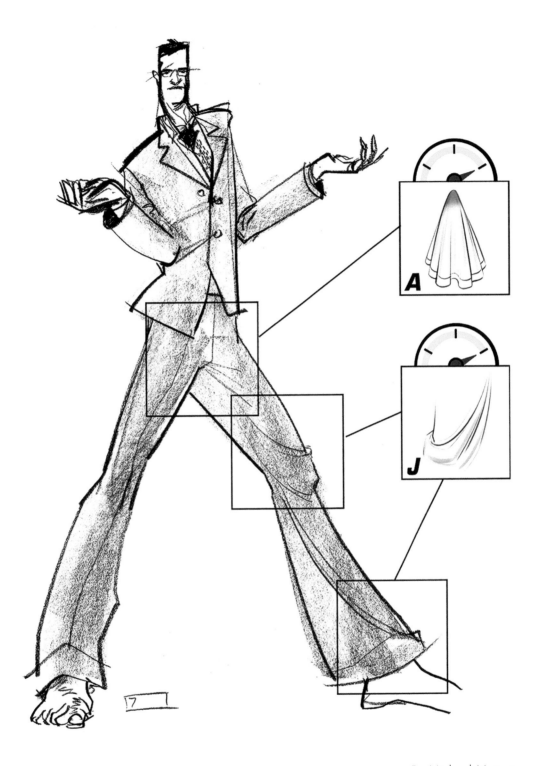

By Michael Mattesi

I show the stiffness of this polyester tuxedo with the lack of folds, and use of very angular lines to create its contours. The A- and J-Folds, and lines, are of medium thickness as well, since this is not a very heavy or thick fabric.

By Michael Mattesi

Observe the texture difference between the sweat jacket, the dress, and the model's skin. These three distinctions show clear contrast and bring so much reality and believability to the drawing! These design decisions were all accomplished in this drawing in 5 minutes, so you are tracking FORCE, form, shape, and textures all at the same time. It sounds like a lot to think about, but in the end, it comes down to being present and sensitive to what you are seeing. How much can you see and feel?

By Michael Mattesi

To push contrast, I give you a knight in metallic armor with sharp points made of steel plates that I drew with Sharpie marker. I wanted a lack of line thickness change for the armor. The cloak hangs from the knight's neck and shoulders with long sweeping U-Folds.

Here is Mritunjay's awesome illustration. I enjoy the lines that show the stiff feel of the jacket in contrast to the more wrinkled pants. The crisp corners of her bags and the rigid edges suggest the stiffness of their paper when carrying the beautiful items, she just purchased. The entire illustration was created with traditional materials. The black line for the clothes was drawn with brush pen and for the arm a Micron was used. All color was painted with granulated watercolors.

By Michael Mattesi

Here, the simplified and powerful FORCE shapes of the thighs give us the Tension FORCE from the rear-end and down the model's left leg. You can feel the heavy and stiff quality of the stitched poncho thrown over the left shoulder of the model

By Michael Mattesi

Let's have a little fun with fashion illustration at the end of our journey. With experience, you discover that you will not need to work through all of the preparation work as we did in the Process chapter of the book. I created this illustration going immediately for the shape design of the jacket and the dress. The strong contrast between the two adds excitement to the image. The silk fabric generates thick, sharp angles at the elbows, and heavy, draping to the bottom of the coat. Design created by John Galliano for Christian Dior.

By Michael Mattesi

I want to take a moment to speak about materials. Almost every drawing in this book was illustrated digitally. As we discussed a few pages earlier, Mritunjay drew his illustration with brush marker, Microns and water color. I created the above illustrations with black India ink and Dr. Martin's Dyes for the hair. I wanted the dress and top to show strong contrast between collected areas of black to thin black lines that would look like lace. I did this by drawing with the tip of the eyedropper that came with the dye and ink.

By Michael Mattesi

Anand Kabra, designer of this Indian Sari, uses much pleating and draping to accomplish the fluidity of the outfit. The dress was made from 20 feet of uncut fabric. This means the designer created the outfit fully from the pleating and draping. Amazing.

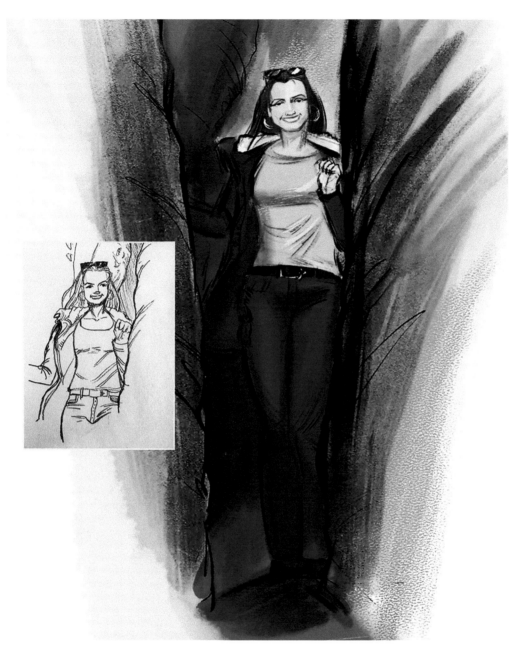

By Michael Mattesi

Marin wears her cotton, coal, parka again with a form-fitting shirt and blue jeans. The stiff parka minimizes fold. I added bumpy texture to the edge of the wool and stiffer lines to the cotton portion of the jacket. The jeans only show subtle folds at the knees since they the present the former bending function of the legs. I added a preliminary line drawing for you to see my study while of line alongside my digital painting.

Now that you have a better understanding of how to draw clothing through FORCE Fabric, you can further dress your drawings with other accessories, all of which will also help show FORCE, form, and shape in your drawing. Here is a brief list for you to consider:

- Anklets
- Toe rings
- Body jewelry
- Chokers
- First Aid gear such as a cast or sling
- Arm warmers
- Shoulder bags
- Backpacks
- Headbands
- Hair clips and barrettes
- Hair bands
- Hair combs
- Hair ties
- Hair pins
- Wigs and hairpieces

- Earmuffs
- Goggles
- Face mask
- Bandannas
- Cufflink
- Sunglasses
- Jewelry
- Ties
- Bow ties
- Pocket squares
- Suspenders
- Handbags, purses, and wallets
- Brooches
- Watches
- Umbrellas

Gravity has a significant effect on clothing, and how it is perceived by the viewer. When clothing is worn on the body, it naturally falls and drapes in response to the pull of gravity. This can create folds and other distortions in the fabric that can add depth and realism to the clothing. In art and animation, depicting the effects of gravity on clothing can help bring characters and costumes to life and make them look more believable. By paying attention to how clothing falls and drapes, artists can create dynamic and realistic designs that accurately reflect the forces at play. In addition, understanding the effects of gravity on clothing can also be useful for costume designers and fashion professionals, who must consider these factors when creating garments that are functional and aesthetically pleasing.

Congratulations. You made it to the end of the FORCE Fabric. I hope you have a better understanding of fabric and how to draw clothing. We have covered a great many subjects beginning with the basics of FORCE, form, and shape, and how all three relate to clothes. Then, you learned about Gravity and Applied FORCE Anchor Points, along with the fold types and how they function. Finally, we covered the three fit types, and the concept of including texture in your work! Now, go and draw models from reference or imagination, and clothe them in the endless options found in fashion. With your newly learned concepts and knowledge of clothes, bring story and believability to your drawings.

Index

Note: *Italic* page numbers refer to figures.